KU-876-433

# THE TUPPERWARE COOK

This book was produced by
Sackville Design Group Limited
Hales Barn
New Street
Stradbroke
Suffolk IP21.5JG

© 1988 Sackville Design Group Limited
and The Tupperware Company
ISBN 0 948615 22 2

All rights reserved. No part of this publication
may be reproduced, stored in a retrieval system,
or transmitted, in any form or by any means,
electronic, mechanical, photocopying,
recording or otherwise, without the prior
written permission of the publishers.

Typeset in Bembo by Halcyon Type and
Design Limited, Ipswich
Printed and bound by William Clowes
Limited, England

Project director: Joan Jackson
Art director: Al Rockall
Designed by: Rolando Ugolini
Edited by: Heather Thomas and Philippa Algeo
Home economist and recipes
created by: Jane Anderson
Photographs by: Barry Bullough, Simon Smith
and Jon Harris

Tupperware products are designed,
researched and kitchen-tested to produce
unique New Products for today's busy
lifestyles. Space saving, time saving, energy
saving, food saving, these are the design
criteria for every New Tupperware product.

Tupperware products are precision made to
the highest standards from the finest
materials and have a 10-year guarantee of
quality.

The Tupperware Company
Tupperware House
130 College Road
Harrow
Middlesex HA1 1BQ

© **Tupperware, TupperWave and Tuppertoys are**
**registered trademarks of Dart Industries Inc.**

# Contents

The Tupperware story 5

Fridge and freezer freshness 7

Be prepared with Tupperware 8

Healthy eating with Tupperware 10

Sauces and dressings 12

Party savouries 14

Buffet dishes 16

Starters 18

Stocks and soups 20

Pastry and savouries 22

Rice cookery 24

Chinese dishes 26

Cooking fish 30

Meals from the microwave 34

Quick meals 38

Vegetables and salads 42

Desserts 50

Cakes and cookies 56

Breakfast 62

Barbecues 64

Picnics 66

Packed lunches 68

Children's dishes 70

Index 72

**Notes to the text:**
In the lists of ingredients measurements are given using Tupperware Metric Measuring Spoons and the Metric Measuring Set cups and 500ml jug. Unless otherwise stated, eggs are size 3.

# The Tupperware Story

The Tupperware contemporary range of products will create space in your home, enhance your kitchen and improve your lifestyle. They are designed specially for modern living, and this beautiful Tupperware cookery book gives you many ideas for the best and most efficient use of your Tupperware products which will last you a lifetime. All the recipes in this book use healthy ingredients to help you feed your family well.

### Tupperware fits your kitchen
Tupperware is a real pace-setter in the kitchen and is colour-coordinated to match any kitchen design or colour scheme.

### Tupperware storage
Tupperware has revolutionised food storage, making effective use of your cupboard space and providing the right containers for this purpose.

### Be prepared with Tupperware
With Tupperware you can prepare in advance and save time and energy. You can even take short-cuts by measuring, preparing, sealing and storing in the same container!

### Serve in Tupperware
Each Tupperware serving plate or dish has its own seal or cover, enabling you to prepare ahead, store and serve at leisure, confident that the food will be really fresh and delicious.

# Fridge and freezer freshness

You can seal in the real flavour and freshness of food with the versatile range of Tupperware containers. They are perfect for storing food in your fridge and freezer. The space-saving designs allow you to make the most effective use of available space.

## Fridge freshness

Make the most of limited fridge space with Tupperware. The containers protect and seal in freshness, keeping salads crisp, vegetables fresh and prolonging the life of many raw and cooked foods.

The sheer Space Saver Bowls and containers give you a clear view of the contents at a glance, saving time too. The exclusive salad products – the Tupperware Space Saver Crisper, Super Crisp-It and Colander – are designed for salad storage, preparation and serving. The Crisper two-level grid drains off excess water, allows air to circulate freely and creates more effective storage space.

## Freezer freshness

The Tupperware Freezer Range protects your food in the freezer. It is designed with all the built-in features you need for successful freezing:

- airtight seals
- sturdy containers
- stackability to save space
- flexibility to –20°C to eliminate cracking
- unique shaping to allow air to circulate and maintain a constant temperature for best food quality

- wide range of shapes and sizes for every need

A well-stocked freezer can be the most valuable asset in every home, for busy mums or working women. You can cook ahead in bulk and freeze what you don't need for future meals.

Many of the Tupperware recipes in this book are suitable for freezing, and you can freeze prepared dishes ready to defrost or reheat in the unique TupperWave Reheatables in your microwave oven. For successful freezing, always follow these simple guidelines:

1 Select foods that are in top condition.
2 Prepare the foods quickly.
3 Vegetables should be blanched and cooled quickly before freezing.
4 Pack the food in Tupperware, seal and label.
5 Freeze quickly and do not overload the fast freezing capacity.

Of course, you can freeze fresh foods as well as cooked dishes. Vegetables, fruit, fish, meat and poultry can all be frozen safely in Tupperware without any significant loss of quality or flavour. If you grow your own vegetables or fruit and have a glut, or buy them in bulk when they are in season, cheap and plentiful, what better way to store them for future enjoyment than in Tupperware in your freezer? In this way, you can enjoy raspberries, blackcurrants and gooseberries at Christmas, asparagus in the autumn, and broad beans in the spring!

# Be prepared with Tupperware

With Tupperware you can prepare with pleasure and ease, store with confidence and serve at your leisure. The comprehensive range of mixing, measuring and preparation products are the right tools for today's busy cook.

Every product is extensively kitchen tested to ensure that all the necessary features are included and to save you time and labour, whether you are preparing family meals or cooking for an important party.

Try making double the quantity of soups, stews, casseroles, pies, cakes, bread and sauces and simply freeze until required. In this way, you will be prepared for any occasion – an impromptu party, unexpected guests, your children's schoolfriends or a quick TV supper.

Multi-functional preparation products like the Mix-N-Stor (featured in the centre of the photograph) enable you to prepare ahead, measure and mix the ingredients, and then seal to store in the same bowl. Short-cuts such as this are invaluable.

The colourful Chop-N-Grate and Cook's Maid will brighten up your kitchen and have a variety of uses. For example, the Cook's Maid (featured in the photograph below) combines an egg separator, juicer and zester which all fit on the same jug and store to-gether as a compact unit. The Chop-N-Grate (featured below left) is the perfect cook's tool. You can snap the inserts into the frame to slice, shred or grate, then the chopping board snaps over the frame for neat storage.

With the Tupperware unique range of products for easy preparation and safe storage, you can solve all your kitchen problems and save time by saving steps.

# Healthy eating with Tupperware

Good healthy wholefoods with nothing added or taken away form the basis of a nutritious diet for you and all your family.

Tupperware can help you enjoy a better and more varied diet as it is ideal for preparing, storing and serving fresh, healthy foods. Eating this way will prevent excessive weight gain and keep you looking slim and feeling fit.

Feeding your children a healthy diet will give them the best possible start in life so that they embark on a lifetime of good eating habits. Try to limit their intake of highly refined convenience foods which sometimes contain artificial additives and may lack health-giving nutrients and natural fibre.

What should you eat? The daily nutrients you need for the maintenance of good health are protein, carbohydrates, vitamins, minerals and some fats. If you regularly eat a balance of fresh fruit, vegetables, whole-grain cereals and bread, beans and pulses, low-fat dairy products, fish, poultry and meat, then you can rest assured that you have a healthy, nutritious diet.

However, most of us eat too many fats, sugars and starchy, over-refined foods and not enough healthy foods and fibre. Fats and sugars lurk hidden in many of the everyday meals and snacks that you eat without you even realising – for instance, in biscuits, cakes, mayonnaise, sauces and pastry.

For a healthy diet, follow these simple guidelines:

● Reduce your intake of fat: eat less butter, cream, full-fat milk and cream, cakes, biscuits, sauces and pastries. Substitute low-fat milk, cheeses and yoghurt and skimmed milk for the full-fat varieties.

● Eat more fibre: eat more wholemeal bread, whole-grain cereals,

muesli, beans, fresh fruit and vegetables.

- Eat less sugar: stop sugaring drinks
and breakfast cereals. Eat fewer
cakes, biscuits, cookies and desserts.
Avoid convenience foods which
may be high in sugar, and
sweetened yoghurts, drinks and
canned fruit in syrup.
- Use less salt: try to substitute
natural flavourings such as herbs
and spices or lemon juice for salt
when possible. Of course, you need
some salt but only in moderation.
Salt to taste instead of salting as a
matter of course.

Follow these easy guidelines and cook
the healthy way with this book, and
you will soon feel healthier, be less
vulnerable to infection, and maybe
even lose some weight as time passes
and healthy eating becomes your way
of life.

# Easy white sauce

15g/½ oz plain or wholemeal flour
15g/½ oz sunflower margarine
300ml/½ pint whole or semi-skimmed milk
salt and freshly ground black pepper

## Method

Place all the ingredients in a Multi Mixing Bowl. Whisk together and pour into a saucepan. Bring to the boil, stirring all the time to thicken. Use as required. To stop a skin forming, seal in a Space Saver Bowl, and leave to cool.

**To freeze:** Make double the quantity. Place in a Tupperware freezer container. Seal, label and freeze.

---

# Sweet and sour sauce

250ml cup/4 oz onion, chopped
1 clove garlic, crushed
15ml/1 tbsp sunflower oil
100ml cup/2 oz red pepper, diced
100ml cup/2 oz green pepper, diced
100ml cup/2 oz carrot strips
15ml/1 tbsp cornflour
300ml/½ pint fresh orange juice
15ml/1 tbsp brown sugar
30ml/2 tbsp rich Soy sauce
dash Tabasco sauce
dash Worcestershire sauce
freshly ground black pepper

## Method

Place the onion and garlic in a pan with the oil and cook for a few minutes to soften. Add the red and green pepper and carrot. Place the cornflour in a Quick Shake, add the orange juice, brown sugar, Soy sauce, Tabasco, Worcestershire sauce and pepper. Shake to blend, then pour into the pan with the vegetables. Bring to the boil, stirring all the time, until thickened and cleared. Use for Chinese food and pork or chicken dishes.

**To freeze:** Make double the quantity, cool and place in Freeze-N-Stor containers. Seal, label and freeze.

# Tomato sauce

15ml/1 tbsp oil
100ml cup/2 oz onion, chopped
1 clove garlic, crushed
500ml jug/1 lb tomatoes,
    skinned or canned
pinch of brown sugar
5ml/1 tsp tomato purée
5ml/1 tsp parsley, chopped

## Method

Place the oil in a saucepan and sauté the onion and garlic until softened. Stir in the remaining ingredients and simmer for about 10 minutes, until the sauce has reduced and thickened.

**To freeze:** Make double the quantity required. Seal, label and freeze half in a Freeze-N-Stor.

**Refrigeration:** Use half straight away and store the remainder in Tupperware in the fridge. Use within 2 days.

---

# Béchamel sauce

450ml/¾ pint milk
1 carrot, roughly chopped
1 small onion, roughly chopped
1 bay leaf
sprig each of fresh parsley, tarragon and
    thyme **or**
5ml/1 tsp mixed herbs
4 black peppercorns
little grated nutmeg
20g/¾ oz butter or sunflower margarine
20g/¾ oz plain or wholemeal flour

## Method

Place the milk in a saucepan, and add the vegetables, bay leaf, herbs, peppercorns and nutmeg. Bring to the boil and pour into a Mix-N-Stor jug and seal. Leave to infuse for 20 minutes. Strain the milk into a clean pan, discarding the vegetables, etc. Make the sauce as described for easy white sauce. Use this sauce for fish, chicken and vegetable dishes.

# Mayonnaise

*2 egg yolks, at room temperature*
*150ml/ ¼ pint olive oil*
*5ml/ 1 tsp wine vinegar or lemon juice*
*2.5ml/ ½ tsp French mustard*
*salt and freshly ground black pepper*

## Method

Place the egg yolks in the Quick Shake and add the olive oil. Seal and shake 10 times. Add the vinegar or lemon juice and mustard and shake once. Season with salt and pepper.

**Alternatively,** place the egg yolks in a Multi Mixing Bowl and beat in the vinegar and mustard using a hand or electric mixer. Then gradually beat in the oil, adding it drop by drop. As the mixture begins to thicken add the oil in a steady stream. Season to taste.

## Variation

**Lemon mayonnaise:** Substitute lemon juice for vinegar. Once made, stir in the juice and grated rind of 1 lemon.

# Yoghurt and mint dressing

*150ml/ ¼ pint natural yoghurt*
*30ml/ 2 tbsp lemon juice*
*salt and freshly ground*
  *black pepper*
*30ml/ 2 tbsp fresh mint,*
  *chopped*
*30ml/ 2 tbsp fresh*
  *parsley, chopped*

## Method

Place all the ingredients in a Quick Shake. Seal and shake until well blended. Use straight away or seal and set aside until needed. Shake again before use.

# Vinaigrette dressing

*150ml/ ¼ pint olive oil*
*30ml/ 2 tbsp wine or herb vinegar*
*salt and freshly ground black pepper*
*1 clove garlic, crushed (optional)*
*30ml/ 2 tbsp parsley, basil or tarragon,*
  *chopped*
*5ml/ 1 tsp French mustard*

## Method

Place all the ingredients in a Quick Shake. Seal and shake until well blended. Use straight away or set aside until needed. Shake again before use.

## Variation

**Orange dressing:** Replace the vinegar with fresh orange juice, omit the mustard and add the chopped flesh of 1 orange.

*Clockwise from the top:* Vinaigrette dressing; Easy white sauce; Tomato sauce; Mayonnaise.

# Party savouries

## Kiwi and prawn triangles

*6 slices Vogel mixed grain bread*
*125g/ 4 oz low fat soft cheese or cream cheese*
*175g/ 6 oz fresh peeled prawns, thawed*
*2 kiwi fruit, peeled and sliced*
*15ml/ 1 tbsp parsley, chopped*

### Method

Toast the bread evenly, cool and spread with the cheese. Cut into triangles. Decorate with the prawns, kiwi fruit and chopped parsley. Makes 20 triangles.

## Pâté and olive pastries

*1 quantity shortcrust pastry (see page 22)*
*1 egg, beaten*
*sprinkling of dried parsley*

Topping:
*250g/ 8 oz smooth chicken liver pâté*
*stuffed olives*
*4 tomatoes, deseeded and sliced*

### Method

Roll the pastry out thinly on the Pastry Sheet. Cut into small shapes using the Cookie Cutter Set. Place on a baking sheet, brush with a little egg, and sprinkle with parsley. Bake at 180° C/350°F/Gas mark 4 for 5-6 minutes. Cool. Spread with pâté and garnish with sliced olive and tomato. Makes 30 pastries.

## Fruity cheese sticks

*½ fresh pineapple*
*250g/ 8 oz Gruyère or mature Cheddar cheese, cubed*
*½ cucumber, cubed*
*125g/ 4 oz black grapes, halved and pipped*

### Method

Cut the pineapple into chunks and thread onto wooden cocktail sticks with cubes of cheese, cucumber and grapes. Makes 16.

*Top left:* Hummus; *top right:* Guacamole avocado dip with crudités; *bottom left, clockwise from the top:* Fruity cheese sticks; Kiwi and prawn triangles; Parma ham and melon on sticks (see page 19); Pâté and olive pastries.

# Guacamole avocado dip

*2 ripe avocados, halved*
*2 tomatoes, skinned, deseeded and chopped*
*15ml/ 1 tbsp lemon juice*
*100ml cup/ 3 oz onion, chopped*
*1 clove garlic, crushed*
*100ml cup/ 3 oz green pepper, chopped*
*5 coriander seeds*
*2 chillis, diced*
*30ml/ 2 tbsp natural yoghurt*
*salt and freshly ground black pepper*
*pinch of sugar*

### Method

Place the avocado, tomato and all the remaining ingredients in a food processor and process until smooth, (alternatively, mash together). Serve in the Serve-It-All, with vegetable sticks (crudités) and savoury crisps. **Serves** 6-8 as a starter or 10 for a party savoury.

# Taramasalata

*125g/ 4 oz smoked cod roe, skinned*
*3 slices stale bread, crusts removed*
*2 cloves garlic, crushed (optional)*
*150ml/ ¼ pint olive oil*
*freshly ground black pepper*
*60ml/ 4 tbsp lemon juice*

### Method

Place the smoked cod roe in a Multi Server, cover with water and soak for 30 minutes. Drain. Soak the bread in water until pulpy. Place the cod roe, bread and all the remaining ingredients in a food processor and blend until thick and creamy. Serve with toast or pitta bread. This is also ideal served on little pastry shapes, garnished with an olive for party savouries.

# Hummus

*175g/6 oz chick peas, soaked overnight*
*juice of 2 large lemons*
*2 cloves garlic, crushed*
*100ml cup/3oz tahini paste (sesame paste)*
*salt and pepper*
*15ml/1 tbsp sesame oil*
*pinch cayenne pepper*

## Method

Drain and cook the chick peas in a pan of fresh hot water until tender. Drain and cool. Place in a food processor or blender with the remaining ingredients and purée. Serve in an Oriental Bowl with a sprinkling of cayenne pepper as a pâté with pitta bread and green salad.

**To freeze:** Place in a Square Round and seal, label and freeze

# Yoghurt and mint dip

*1 large cucumber, peeled and diced*
*3 spring onions, chopped*
*15ml/1 tbsp fresh dill or parsley, chopped*
*30ml/2 tbsp fresh mint, chopped*
*300ml/½ pint natural Greek yoghurt*
*salt and freshly ground black pepper*
*5ml/1 tsp lemon juice*

## Method

Place the cucumber in a Multi Server and sprinkle with salt. Leave for 15 minutes, rinse well, drain and pat dry on kitchen paper. Mix the cucumber, onions and herbs into the yoghurt. Season well, and add the lemon juice. Serve chilled with salad and warmed pitta bread. **Serves:** 6-8 as a starter or 10 for a party savoury.

## Mint chocolate mousses

175g/ 6 oz plain chocolate
6 eggs, size 3, separated
300ml/ ½ pint double cream
10ml/ 2 tsp mint liquor
50g/ 2 oz chocolate mint matchsticks, broken
150ml/ ¼ pint double cream
sugared mint leaves for decoration

### Method

Melt the chocolate in a Tupperware Multi Server (see page 51). Stir the egg yolks into the chocolate. Whip the cream until thick in a Mix-N-Stor, with the outer rim fitted.

Fold the cream into the chocolate, with the mint liquor and matchsticks. Whisk the egg whites until stiff in a Multi Mixing Bowl . Fold into the chocolate mixture thoroughly. Spoon into 8 pots.

Refrigerate until set.

Whip the remaining cream and pipe into rosettes and place a sugared mint leaf on each one. **Serves** 8.

### Sugared leaves

Brush the mint leaves with a little egg white and dip in caster sugar. Leave for an hour and repeat. Use to decorate puddings.

## Summer fruit cheesecake

1 sachet of Quick-Jel
225g/ 8 oz fruit compôte of cooked fruit
2 eggs, size 3, separated
200g/ 7 oz cream cheese
125g/ 4 oz cottage cheese
75g/ 3 oz caster sugar
grated rind and juice 1 lemon
15g/ ½ oz gelatine
75ml/ 3 tbsp boiling water
300ml/ ½ pint raspberry fromage frais
250g/ 8 oz almond biscuits, crushed
125g/ 4 oz melted butter

### Method

Make up the Quick-Jel according to the instructions on the packet, using any fruit juice as liquid. Place the fruit in the base of a 1.5 litre Jel-Ring. Cover with the Quick-Jel and refrigerate until set.

Beat together the egg yolks, cheese, sugar, and lemon. Dissolve the gelatine in the water and fold carefully into the cream mixture. Fold in the fromage frais. Whisk the egg whites until softly stiff and fold into the cream cheese mixture. Spoon into the Jel-Ring and refrigerate until set. Mix the biscuits with the melted butter and carefully spread over the cheesecake. Seal and refrigerate for 2 hours.

To serve, remove the seal and cover with a Serve-It-All plate. Invert and then remove the inner seal, easing it away carefully. Then remove the Jel-Ring itself. Decorate with whipped cream and fresh fruit as desired. **Serves** 6-8.

### Cook's tip

Cook and freeze summer soft fruit in small

portions in Square Rounds. Use for desserts, pies, trifle and other puddings.

—❧—

## Lemon salmon in filo pastry

*4 salmon steaks*
*125g/ 4 oz butter, softened*
*15ml/ 1 tbsp fennel, chopped*
*15ml/ 1 tbsp parsley, chopped*
*5ml/ 1 tsp lemon rind*
*12 sheets filo pastry*
*25g/ 1 oz melted butter*

### Method
Remove the skin from the salmon and the centre bone. Divide each steak into 4 portions, making 16. Mix the butter, fennel, parsley and lemon in a Multi Mixing Bowl.

With all the sheets of filo pastry on top of each other, cut into quarters. Using 3 sheets of pastry together place a piece of

*Above:* Summer fruit cheesecake.

salmon in the centre and spread some of the herb butter on top. Bring the corners of the pastry together with a twist at the top, seal and brush with the melted butter. Repeat to make 16.

Place on a greased baking sheet and bake in a preheated oven 200°C/400°F/Gas mark 6 for 15-20 minutes until golden. Serve warm or cold as part of a buffet party spread. **Makes** 16.

—❧—

## Onion and sour cream dip

*1 packet of dry onion soup mix*
*125ml/ 4 fl oz natural yoghurt*
*125ml/ 4 fl oz soured cream*
*15ml/ 1 tbsp parsley, chopped*

### Method
Whisk all the ingredients together and serve in an Oriental Twin.

17

# Tuna mousse

40g/ 1½ oz powdered gelatine
150ml/ ¼ pint hot water
¼ cucumber, thinly sliced
200g/ 7 oz canned tuna, drained and flaked
200ml/ 7 fl oz mayonnaise
grated rind and juice of 1 lemon
15ml/ 1 tbsp parsley or chives, chopped
salt and pepper
300ml/ ½ pint double cream, lightly
 whipped
3 egg whites, stiffly beaten

To garnish:
tomato slices, black olives and lettuce

## Method
Sprinkle the gelatine on to the hot water and stir gently until dissolved. Cool a little and pour about 20ml into the base of a 1.5 litre Jel-Ring, rotating the mould to cover the bottom with a thin layer. Arrange the cucumber in overlapping slices in the base and place in the refrigerator until set.

Meanwhile, mix the tuna, mayonnaise, lemon juice and rind, chives and seasoning in a 3.0 litre Multi Mixing Bowl until smooth and creamy, using an electric whisk. Add the remaining gelatine mixture and stand in a cool place until the mousse starts to set. Fold in the whipped cream and egg whites, and pour into the Jel-Ring. Seal and chill until set.

To turn out, remove the seal and invert onto the shallow plate of the Serve-It-All. Gently remove the centre seal and then the ring. Place the plate on the pedestal, fill the centre with sliced tomato and garnish the border with tomato, olives and lettuce. **Serves** 6-8.

# Marinated mushroom starter

250g/ 8 oz tiny button mushrooms
100ml/ 7 tbsp walnut oil
100ml/ 7 tbsp cider vinegar
2.5ml/ ½ tsp dry English mustard
pinch dried tarragon
100ml/ 7 tbsp port or red wine
pinch salt and freshly gound black pepper
30ml/ 2 tbsp parsley, chopped
1ml/ ¼ tsp brown sugar, optional

To garnish:
lettuce leaves and 4 walnut halves

## Method
Wash the button mushrooms and pat dry on kitchen paper. Place in a Space Saver Bowl. Place the remaining ingredients in a Quick Shake container, cover, seal and

shake a few times. Pour the dressing over the mushrooms. Cover and seal and shake the bowl once. Refrigerate for 3 hours, giving the bowl a shake occasionally. Serve on a bed of lettuce, garnished with walnuts in individual dishes, with wholemeal bread. **Serves** 4.

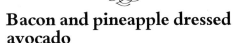

## Bacon and pineapple dressed avocado

*125g/4 oz back bacon*
*200g/7.5 oz soft cream cheese*
*4 sprigs fresh parsley*
*1 clove garlic*
*250ml cup/4 oz pineapple pieces*
*salt and freshly ground black pepper*
*dash Tabasco sauce*
*3 avocados*
*parsley to garnish*
*6-12 slices of Vogel bread, toasted*

### Method
Grill the bacon rashers until crisp. Trim off the crispy ends and reserve. Place the remaining bacon, cream cheese, parsley, garlic and pineapple in a food processor or blender. Process until smooth. Add the salt, pepper and Tabasco to taste. Place in a Cereal Bowl, seal and refrigerate for 30 minutes or until required.

Halve the avocados and remove the stones. Arrange on a serving plate and divide the bacon and pineapple dressing between them. Garnish each with a piece of the reserved crisp bacon and parsley. Serve with triangles of toast. **Serves** 6.

## Parma ham and fruit on sticks

*½ Ogen melon, skinned and deseeded*
*8 thin slices of Parma ham*
*1 ripe mango, peeled and stoned*
*125g/4 oz Mozzarella cheese, cubed*
*1 bunch fresh watercress*

### Method
Slice the melon into 8 wedges, wrap each in a slice of ham, and cut in half. Cut the mango into large pieces. Thread the melon and ham, mango and cheese alternately on to wooden cocktail sticks, allowing 2 sticks per person. Arrange on a Square Server.

Pick over the watercress and place in a Colander, rinse thoroughly under cold running water and drain. Garnish the savoury sticks with plenty of watercress. Cover and refrigerate until required. **Serves** 4.

*Below left to right:* Tuna mousse; Marinated mushroom starter; Bacon and pineapple dressed avocado; Parma ham and fruit on sticks.

## Basic chicken stock

*chicken bones from roast chicken or chicken
    portions*
*2 carrots, roughly chopped*
*1 onion, roughly chopped*
*pinch of salt*
*freshly ground black pepper*

**Method**
Place all the ingredients in a large saucepan
and cover with plenty of cold water. Bring
to the boil, cover and simmer for about one
hour. Cool and strain into Freeze-N-Stors.
Label and store for up to 2 months in a 4
star freezer cabinet.

## Basic fish stock

*1kg/2 lb white fish bones, head and
    trimmings*
*1 onion, roughly chopped*
*1 carrot, roughly chopped*
*sprigs of fresh herbs (parsley, thyme and
    tarragon)* **or**
*1 bouquet garni*
*pinch of salt*
*freshly ground black pepper*

**Method**
Place all the ingredients in a large saucepan
and cover with plenty of cold water. Bring
to the boil and simmer gently for 30-40
minutes. Strain into a jug and cool.

**To freeze:** pour into Freeze-N-Stors, seal,
label and freeze. Store for up to 2 months in
a 4 star freezer cabinet.

## Cucumber and yoghurt soup

*1 cucumber, roughly sliced*
*3 spring onions, chopped*
*600ml/1 pint live natural yoghurt*
*30ml/2 tbsp lemon juice*
*45ml/3 tbsp fresh mint, chopped*
*15ml/1 tbsp fresh dill or parsley, chopped*
*salt and freshly ground black pepper*
*pinch of coriander seeds*

**Method**
Place all the ingredients in a food processor
or blender and blend until smooth.
Transfer to a Tupperware bowl, seal and
chill in the refrigerator. Garnish with mint
or parsley. **Serves** 4.

## Special seafood soup

*2 carrots, chopped*
*1 leek, chopped*
*2 cloves garlic, finely chopped*
*2 tomatoes, peeled, deseeded and chopped*
*30ml/2 tbsp olive oil*
*1 onion, chopped*
*250g/8 oz monkfish steak or other firm
    white fish (eg cod)*
*250g/8 oz red mullet*
*8 whole prawns*
*2 small potatoes, peeled and quartered*
*2 sprigs fresh parsley*
*salt and freshly ground black pepper*
*250ml cup/6 oz star pasta for soup*
*pinch of turmeric*
*250ml cup/4 oz grated Gruyère or
    Parmesan cheese*

**Method**
Cook the carrots, leek, garlic and tomatoes
in a large pan with the olive oil for about 5
minutes. Add the onion, monkfish, red
mullet, prawns, potatoes and parsley. Pour
in 1 litre/2 pints water. Season with a little
salt and pepper. Bring to the boil, cover and
simmer for 30 minutes.

Remove a few of the large bones, then
purée the soup in two batches in a food
processor or blender. Strain the liquid back
into the pan, discarding the pulp etc. Stir in
the pasta and turmeric and cook until the
pasta is soft. Taste and adjust the seasoning.
Serve with a sprinkling of grated cheese or
Parmesan, and crusty bread.

**To freeze:** Make double the amount
without the pasta. Place in a Freeze-N-
Stor, label and freeze. Reheat, add the pasta
and simmer until tender.

## Vegetable broth

2 x 250ml cups/8 oz dried haricot beans
30ml/2 tbsp olive oil
250ml cup/4 oz onion, chopped
1 clove garlic, chopped
250ml cup/4 oz carrot, chopped
250ml cup/4 oz French or runner beans,
  chopped
4 tomatoes, peeled and chopped
bouquet garni
sprig of fresh parsley
salt and freshly ground pepper
250ml cup/4 oz grated Guyère or Parmesan
  cheese

### Method
Soak the haricot beans overnight in a Multi Server, completely covering the beans with cold water. Discard the water, place the beans in a pan and cover with fresh

*Above right:* Cucumber and yoghurt soup; *above left:* Vegetable broth.

water. Bring to the boil and simmer for one hour. Drain.

Heat the olive oil in a large pan and add the onion, garlic, carrot, green beans, haricot beans and tomatoes. Cover with 900ml/1½ pints cold water. Add the bouquet garni, parsley and seasoning. Bring to the boil and simmer gently for 45 minutes. Taste and adjust the seasoning.

Use the Chop-N-Grate to grate a sprinkling of cheese over each portion.
**Serves** 4-6.

**To freeze:** Either freeze part or all of the soup in a Freeze-N-Stor or in Square Rounds. Defrost and reheat as required, either in a pan, or in a microwave oven for 3 minutes.

## Wholemeal shortcrust pastry

*300g/10 oz self-raising wholemeal flour*
*pinch of salt*
*150g/5 oz sunflower margarine*
*90ml/6 tbsp cold water*

### Method
Place the flour and salt in a Mix-N-Stor. Add the margarine, place the rim cover on the bowl and mix in the fat with a fork. Alternatively, use your finger tips and rub in in the usual way. (The pastry may be covered with the rim lid, sealed and refrigerated at this stage until required). Stir in the water until the pastry begins to hold together. Form into a dough with your fingers. Knead lightly and use as required. This quantity is sufficient for a large pie or 6 pasties.

---

## Savoury plain pastry

*300g/10 oz plain flour*
*pinch of salt*
*150g/5 oz sunflower margarine*
*60-90ml/4-6 tbsp cold water*

### Method
Make the pastry in the same way as that described for wholemeal pastry. Use as required.

**To freeze:** Roll out into an oblong and place in a Freeze-N-Stor container. Seal, label and freeze.

### Variations
### Cheese pastry
*75g/3 oz cheese, grated*
*pinch of paprika pepper*

### Herb pastry
*45ml/3 tbsp parsley,*
*chopped*

### Horseradish pastry
*30ml/2 tbsp horseradish sauce*
### Method
In all these variations add the extra ingredients before the water.

---

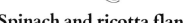

## Spinach and ricotta flan

*1 quantity wholemeal pastry*
*1 onion, chopped*
*1 clove garlic, crushed*
*15ml/1 tbsp sunflower oil*
*500g/1 lb frozen chopped spinach, drained*
*250g/8 oz ricotta or curd cheese*
*salt and freshly ground black pepper*
*2 size 2 eggs, beaten*
*30ml/2 tbsp milk*
*pinch of nutmeg*

### Method
Roll out the pastry on a Pastry Sheet to a circle, about 25-28cm/10-11 in diameter. Use to line a 20-23cm/8-9in flan ring. Bake blind for 10 minutes at 190°C/ 375° F/Gas mark 5. Cook the onion and garlic in the oil to soften. Add the spinach and cheese. Season well. Spread the spinach filling in the base

of the flan ring. Beat the egg, milk and nutmeg together and pour into the flan. Bake at 200°C/400°F/Gas mark 6 for 20-30 minutes. Serve warm with a baked jacket potato or chilled with salad. **Serves 4-6.**

## Leek, mushroom and Mozzarella plait

*1 quantity wholemeal pastry*

Filling:
*1 leek, chopped*
*10 button mushrooms*
*150g/5 oz Mozzarella cheese, sliced*
*3 sprigs of fresh parsley*
*5ml/1 tsp dry English mustard*
*1 egg, beaten*
*salt and freshly ground black pepper*
*4 dashes of Tabasco sauce*

### Method
Roll the pastry out on a Pastry Sheet with a Rolling Pin filled with cold water, until it is approximately 30cm/12in square and trim the edges.

Blend all the filling ingredients in a food processor or liquidizer until smooth. Spread the filling down the centre one-third of the pastry. Cut an equal number of 1½cm/½in strips, obliquely, on each side of the pastry. Fold in both ends and plait alternate strips over filling. Glaze with egg. Use the pastry trimmings for decoration and then glaze. Place the plait carefully on a baking tray and bake in a preheated oven at 180°C, 350°F, Gas mark 4 for 25-30 minutes. Serve hot or cold on the Buffet Server. **Serves 4-6.**

**To freeze:** Cool thoroughly. Slice and freeze in a Freeze-N-Stor container.

Leek, mushroom and Mozzarella plait with Tupperware baking utensils.

# Cooking rice in the Multi Server

**1** Fill the outer bowl of the Multi Server with 1 litre/1¾ pints water. Place the water in a pan and bring to the boil. Add a pinch of salt and 250ml cup/8 oz white rice and stir. Bring back to the boil and simmer for 5 minutes.

Turn the rice and boiling water into the Multi Server colander in the bowl.

**2** Cover and leave undisturbed for 20 minutes.

**3** Lift the colander to drain the rice and pour away the starch-filled water.

**4** Add 450ml/¾ pint hot water to the bowl, replace the colander of rice and cover to keep hot for serving.

The cooked rice can also be used for other recipes.

## Cooking brown rice

Brown rice can be cooked successfully in this way. Boil for 6 minutes and leave covered in the Multi Server for 30 minutes. Easy-cook brown rice, which is readily available, cooks particularly well in this way.

Savoury chicken risotto.

# Savoury chicken risotto

*250ml cup/ 8 oz Easy-cook Italian brown*
*rice or white rice*
*300ml/ ½ pint chicken stock*
*600ml/ 1¼ pints cold water*
*30ml/ 2 tbsp olive oil*
*1 onion, chopped*
*1 clove garlic, crushed*
*125g/ 4 oz back bacon, chopped*
*2 chicken breasts, diced*
*125g/ 4 oz button mushrooms*
*2 courgettes, chopped*
*1 red pepper, chopped*
*15ml/ 1 tbsp parsley, chopped*
*5ml/ 1 tsp paprika pepper*
*salt and freshly ground black pepper*

**Method**
Place the rice in a pan with the chicken stock and cold water. Bring to the boil and cook gently for 5 minutes. Pour the rice and boiling water into the Multi Server colander in the bowl. Cover and leave undisturbed for 20 minutes (allow 25-30 minutes for brown rice).

Heat the oil in a frying pan and cook the onion, garlic and bacon for a few minutes. Stir in the chicken, mushrooms, courgettes and pepper. Cover and cook gently for 10-15 minutes until the chicken is cooked.

Drain the rice and add to the chicken. Stir well, adding the parsley, paprika and seasoning. (Any chopped fresh vegetables can be added, and cooked chicken can also be used.) Serve immediately. **Serves** 4.

# Vegetable and prawn stir-fry

*1 green pepper*
*1 red pepper*
*2 large carrots*
*4 large spring onions, sliced diagonally*
*125g/ 4 oz baby sweetcorn, halved*
*4 radishes, sliced*
*175g/ 6 oz peeled prawns, thawed*
*25ml/ 5 tsp cornflour*
*30ml/ 2 tbsp rich Soy sauce*
*15ml/ 1 tbsp clear honey*
*15ml/ 1 tbsp dry sherry*
*75g/ 3 oz cashew nuts*
*30ml/ 2 tbsp sunflower oil*

## Method

Cut the peppers into wide strips and then into triangular pieces. Halve the carrots lengthways and slice diagonally. Lay all the prepared vegetables and prawns in a Rectangular Server, cover and refrigerate until required. Mix the sauce ingredients together in a Quick Shake and set aside.

Brown the cashew nuts in the hot oil in a wok or a large frying pan. Add the vegetables and stir, cooking quickly over a high heat for about 1 minute. Stir in the prawns. Shake the sauce, shake again and stir into the vegetables. **Serves** 4.

# Crispy pork with water chestnuts and sweet and sour sauce

*60ml/ 4 tbsp cornflour*
*5ml/ 1 tsp salt*
*pinch of baking powder*
*1 size 3 egg, beaten*
*250g/ 8 oz lean pork, cubed*
*oil for frying*
*225g/ 7½ oz can water chestnuts, drained*
*1 quantity sweet and sour sauce (page 12)*

## Method

Mix the cornflour, salt and baking powder together in a Tupperware bowl. Beat the egg with a little water in a separate bowl. Toss the meat in the cornflour, shake off any excess, and coat in the egg. Toss in the cornflour again. Deep fry the pork for 3 minutes until golden in batches. Drain. Mix together with the water chestnuts and hot sweet and sour sauce. **Serves** 4.

# Hot tossed rice

*250ml cup/6 oz easy-cook white rice*
*45ml/3 tbsp sunflower oil*
*3 spring onions, chopped*
*250ml/8 oz fresh root ginger, chopped*
*2 eggs, beaten*
*30ml/2 tbsp light Soy sauce*
*15ml/1 tbsp dry sherry*
*125g/4 oz fresh bean sprouts, soaked*

## Method
Cook the rice in the Multi Server (see page 24). Heat the oil in a wok or large frying pan. Add the onions and ginger and cook for a few seconds. Shake the eggs, Soy sauce and sherry in a Quick Shake and pour into the wok. Stir constantly until the egg is softly cooked. Add the rice and stir well to heat through. Drain the bean sprouts and stir into the rice. **Serves** 4.

*From left to right, top:* Vegetable and prawn stir-fry; Shredded beef with ginger; *right:* Hot tossed rice; *below:* Sweet and sour sauce and Crispy pork with water chestnuts.

# Shredded beef with ginger

*500g/1 lb quick-fry steak, rump steak or skirt of beef*
*30ml/2 tbsp cornflour*
*5ml/1 tsp salt*
*60-90ml/4-6 tbsp sunflower oil*
*60ml/4 tbsp Hoi Sin (barbecue) sauce*
*15ml/1 tbsp dry sherry*
*30ml/2 tbsp fresh green ginger, shredded*
*2 green peppers, seeded and cut into strips*

## Method
Cut the beef into thin slices, cutting across the grain. Coat in a little oil and then toss in the cornflour and salt, in a sealed bowl.

Heat the remaining oil in a wok or a large frying pan. When very hot, throw in the beef and stir vigorously for 1-2 minutes to brown. Add the Hoi Sin sauce and sherry and stir for 1 minute. Stir in the ginger and pepper and heat through for a few seconds. Serve immediately. **Serves** 4.

# Chicken with almonds

*4 chicken breasts, sliced thinly*
*30ml/ 2 tbsp cornflour*
*30ml/ 2 tbsp sunflower oil*
*2 cloves garlic, chopped*
*125g/ 4 oz almonds*
*30ml/ 1 tbsp sugar*
*5ml/ 1 tsp light soy sauce*
*15ml/ 1 tbsp sherry*
*15ml/ 1 tbsp sesame oil*
*6 spring onion curls*

## Method

Coat the chicken in the cornflour. Heat the oil in a wok or large frying pan. Add the chicken and garlic and cook for 3-4 minutes turning all the time. Add the almonds and cook for 1-2 minutes until golden brown.

Blend all the sauce ingredients in a Quick Shake. Stir into the chicken and cook for 1-2 minutes, stirring all the time. Garnish with spring onion tassles. Serve with medium noodles. **Serves** 4.

# Oriental spare ribs

*15ml/ 1 tbsp cornflour*
*100ml/ 7 heaped tbsp barbecue sauce*
*50ml/ 3½ tbsp dry sherry*
*50ml/ 3½ tbsp sesame oil*
*750g/ 1½ lb pork spare ribs, chopped*
*6 spring onions, sliced diagonally*
*1 green pepper, cut into triangles*

## Method

Blend all the sauce ingredients in a Quick Shake. Place the ribs in a Tupperware container and pour the sauce over. Cover and refrigerate for an hour or longer.

Transfer to a baking dish and cook covered for ½ hour at 200°C/400°F/Gas mark 6, and then uncover and add the onions and peppers. Cook for 10 minutes. Serve with salad and noodles or as part of a Chinese meal. **Serves** 4.

### Radish flowers

Cut slits in the top of a radish and chill in cold water to open slightly.

### Spring onion curls

Trim the onions and shred each end into strips lengthways, leaving the middle intact. Place in a bowl filled with iced water. Refrigerate until the ends curl up.

**Carrot shapes**

**Flowers:** Peel and scrape the carrots. Cut strips along the sides of the carrots at regular intervals. Slice horizontally into rings.

**Curls:** Slice the carrots into thin slivers using a potato peeler and use the curls to decorate a dish.

*Top:* Oriental spare ribs; *above:* Chicken with almonds.

**Tomato roses**

Peel a tomato in a continuous strip like an apple. Roll the strip of skin up to look like a rose.

# Poaching fish in the Multi Server

In the bowl, put a sliced carrot, sliced onion, bay leaf, sprigs of thyme and parsley, a lemon slice, salt and peppercorns. Set the colander in the bowl.

**1** Rinse the fish gently in warm water if it is taken from the refrigerator. Place the fish steaks in the colander. Pour boiling water down the side of the bowl, not onto the fish, sufficient just to cover the fish.

**2** Cover and leave undisturbed for 20 minutes. Lift the colander to drain the fish thoroughly. (Use the stock for soups and sauces.) To turn out the steaks easily and perfectly, fit a small plate into the colander and invert the fish onto the plate. Then cover with the Serving Plate and invert again – it is so easy. Arrange and garnish simply.

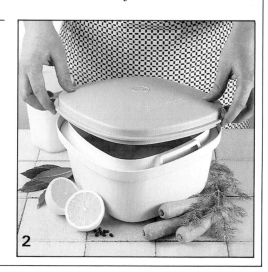

## Cornish fish pie

*Above:* Cornish fish pie.

*3 leeks sliced*
*25g/1 oz butter or sunflower margarine*
*25g/1 oz plain or wholewheat flour*
*cooking liquor from poached fish*
*120ml/4 fl oz thick cream*
*salt and freshly ground black pepper*
*4 poached cod or haddock steaks*
*1 kg/2 lb potatoes*
*milk and butter to mix*

### Method

Sauté the leeks in the butter until just tender. Remove and add the flour. Cook the roux for a couple of minutes but do not allow to brown. Gradually add about 300ml/½ pint of the reserved fish stock, stirring until the sauce is thick and smooth. Stir in the cream and season to taste. Gently break the fish up into chunks and add the sauce with the leeks. Pour into an ovenproof dish.

Cook the potatoes and drain. Mash with enough milk and butter to get a firm but smooth texture. Season to taste. Place in a piping bag and pipe on top of the fish in large swirls. Cook in a preheated oven at 200°C/400°F/Gas mark 6 for 15-20 minutes, or until golden brown. **Serves** 4.

## Poaching fish in the Tupperware Poacher

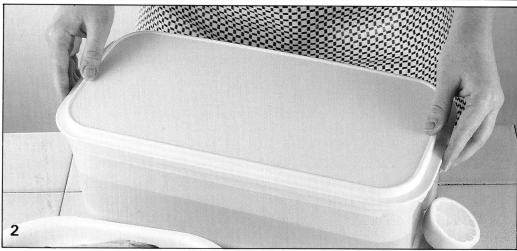

Use the Buffet Server Tray and the Space Saver Crisper to create this useful poacher for poaching fillets of cod, haddock, and whole fish such as salmon, trout, brill and halibut. The liquid used can be plain water, fish stock or a court bouillon. The liquid should only just cover the fish. If using plain water, add 5ml/1 tsp salt per 1 litre/2 pints. If the fish is smoked, do not add salt.

### Poaching a whole salmon

The salmon should not be more than about 30cm/12in in length. This will probably mean that the head will need to be removed before cooking.

### Method

**1** Place the fish on the Crisper Grid with some bay leaves. Pour in the boiling water at the side, not directly onto the fish, just to cover the fish. Add the salt.

**2** Cover with the Buffet Server Tray and leave undisturbed for 40-45 minutes.

**3** Lift the salmon out on the Crisper Grid, drain and place on a board.

**4** Carefully remove the skin from both sides, turning the salmon over very carefully. Ease the bones away by sliding a knife between the bone and flesh on the open side. Do this on both sides. Lift away

**3**

**4**

the bones. Reshape the salmon and lay on the tray of the Buffet Server. Decorate with piped mayonnaise, sliced cucumber, dill or parsley leaves and tomato shapes.

Serve as part of a party buffet spread with salads and other meats. **Serves** 10-12.

## Poaching trout

*2 rainbow trout, approximately 350g/*
    *12 oz each*
*boiling water*
*5ml/1 tsp salt*

**Method**

Gut and descale the fish and wash thoroughly. The fishmonger will usually do this if asked.

Follow the instructions 1-3 for poaching salmon, but leave covered for only 15 minutes, or 12 minutes for smaller fish.

When cooked, lift out the Grid and drain. Remove the heads if wished before serving, and also the bone, or leave whole.

Serve with boiled parsley potatoes, horseradish mayonnaise and salad.

## TupperWave
## Meals from the freezer

All the following recipes can be frozen in the new TupperWave dishes, and then reheated in a microwave oven. Prepare the food in advance, or make double the quantity needed for eating now and freeze half for a later date. TupperWave containers have been designed exclusively for reheating foods in a microwave oven to 150°C. The container and cover are a smokey colour for elegant serving, and for you to see what is happening inside during cooking. The cover fits easily and a step inside the handle creates a vent for steam that builds up in microwave cooking. Turn the cover over and it can be used as a plate for serving. A separate seal is provided so that food can be sealed in for freshness and freezing, and the seal is replaced by the cover for reheating.

*From left to right:* Spicy lamb with caraway dumplings; Red cabbage; Chicken with peppers; Honey and almond pudding (recipe page 36).

# Chicken with peppers

*30ml/2 tbsp oil*
*2 small onions, chopped*
*1 green pepper, seeded and sliced*
*5ml/1 tsp mixed herbs*
*3 chicken breasts, skinned*
*250g/8 oz canned chopped tomatoes*
*150ml/¼ pint red wine*
*150ml/¼ pint water*
*salt and freshly ground black pepper*
*60ml/4 tbsp small pasta shells*
*chopped parsley to garnish*

### Method

Heat the oil in an ovenproof casserole, add the onions and pepper and cook for 3-4 minutes until soft. Press the herbs onto the chicken, add to the pan and brown all over. Add the remaining ingredients and bring to a simmer. Cover and cook in a preheated oven at 200°C/400°F/Gas mark 6 for 45 minutes. **Serves** 4.

**To freeze:** Allow to cool. Place in a 1 litre TupperWave container. Seal, label and freeze for up to 4 months.

**To microwave reheat:** Replace the seal with the TupperWave cover, heat on 50% defrost for 8 minutes, allow to stand for 5 minutes. Heat on full for 4 minutes.

## Spicy lamb with caraway dumplings

*15ml/1 tbsp oil*
*2 large onions, chopped*
*1 clove garlic, chopped*
*1kg/2 lb lamb fillet, diced*
*25g/1 oz wholewheat flour*
*5ml/1 tsp ground cumin*
*2.5ml/½ tsp ground allspice*
*30ml/2 tbsp tomato purée*
*1 bay leaf*
*300ml/½ pint stock*
*salt and freshly ground black pepper*

Dumplings:
*125g/4 oz self-raising flour, wholemeal or white*
*2.5ml/½ tsp salt*
*10ml/2 tsp caraway seeds*
*50g/2 oz shredded suet*
*cold water to mix*

**Method**
Heat the oil in a large ovenproof casserole. Add the onions and garlic, cover and cook for 3 minutes. Add the diced lamb and brown on all sides. Sprinkle the flour over the meat, stir and cook for 1 minute. Gradually add the stock then the seasonings. Heat until simmering then cover and cook for 1 hour in a preheated oven at 180° C/350°F/Gas mark 4.

Prepare the dumplings by combining all the dry ingredients and then adding sufficient cold water to make a manageable soft dough. Lightly knead the dough and divide into 8 pieces, forming each into a ball. Drop the dumplings into the top of the casserole, cover and cook for a further 30 minutes. Adjust the seasoning if necessary. **Serves** 4.

**To freeze:** Do not add the dumplings, allow to cool. Place in a TupperWave 1 litre container, seal and freeze for up to 3 months.

**To microwave reheat:** Add the dumplings, replace the seal with the cover, and heat for 15-20 minutes. Stir 4-5 times for even defrosting and heating.

# Chillied beef and kidney beans

*500g/1 lb minced beef*
*50g/2 oz brown breadcrumbs*
*1 clove garlic, chopped*
*15ml/1 tbsp tomato purée*
*10ml/2 tsp chilli powder*
*5ml/1 tsp paprika pepper*
*439g/15 oz can chopped tomatoes*
*439g/15 oz can kidney beans*
*2.5ml-5ml/½-1 tsp chilli powder*
*2.5ml/½ tsp cumin powder*
*10ml/2 tsp cornflour*
*30ml/2 tbsp red wine*
*pinch dried thyme*
*salt and freshly ground black pepper*
*142ml/5 fl oz soured cream*

## Method

Blend the beef, breadcrumbs, garlic, tomato purée, chilli powder and paprika. Shape into 14 small meat balls. Place in a shallow, ovenproof dish, cover and bake in a preheated oven at 200°C/400°F/Gas mark 6 for 30 minutes.

Mix the tomatoes, kidney beans, chilli and cumin powder in a saucepan. Blend the cornflour and wine. Stir into the tomato mixture and season well with thyme, salt and pepper. Bring to the boil to thicken, and simmer for 5 minutes, stirring occasionally. Serve the meatballs in the sauce with a spoonful of soured cream on each portion. **Serves** 4.

**To freeze:** Place the meatballs and sauce in a 1 litre TupperWave container. Seal, label and freeze.

**To microwave reheat:** Defrost in the microwave on low. Reheat in the microwave for 6 minutes on high.

The following dessert recipes can be prepared quickly and easily in the TupperWave containers in the microwave oven.

# Pear and cinnamon crumble

*1kg/2 lb conference pears, peeled chopped*
*    and cooked*
*50g/2 oz brown sugar*
*2.5ml/½ tsp nutmeg*
*250g/8 oz raspberries*
*25g/1 oz butter*
*125g/4 oz wholemeal breadcrumbs*
*50g/2 oz soft brown sugar*
*5ml/1 tsp cinnamon*
*150ml/¼ pint crème fraîche*

## Method

Mix the pears with the sugar and nutmeg, and layer with the raspberries in a 750ml TupperWave container. Leave aside.

Mix the butter with the breadcrumbs, sugar and cinnamon and cook in a saucepan for 4-5 minutes, stirring occasionally. Spread the breadcrumbs over the cooked fruit and reheat for 1 minute on high in the microwave oven. Serve straight away with crème fraîche.
**Serves** 6.

# Honey and almond pudding

*50g/2 oz sunflower margarine*
*50g/2 oz caster sugar*
*50g/2 oz wholemeal self-raising flour*
*1 egg, size 3*
*15ml/1 tbsp clear honey*
Topping:
*15ml/1 tbsp clear honey*
*125g/4 oz fromage frais*
*50g/2 oz flaked almonds, toasted*

## Method

Beat together the margarine, sugar, flour, egg and honey. Spoon into a 500ml TupperWave container. Smooth over. Cook in a microwave oven on high, uncovered, for 3 minutes. Spread the honey over the top, cover with the fromage frais and sprinkle with almonds. **Serves** 4.

*Top:* Pear and cinnamon crumble; *below:* Spicy beef and kidney beans.

## Pizza bread base

*300g/ 10 oz bread mix*
*200ml/ 7 fl oz hand-hot water*

### Method
Place the bread mix in a Multi Mixing Bowl. Add the water and mix to a dough. Knead lightly on a floured Pastry Sheet for about 4-5 minutes. Shape into 2 20cm/8 in circles. Place on a greased baking tray. Leave to prove in a warm place for 25 minutes. Spread the chosen topping onto the base. Bake in a preheated oven at 220° C/425°F/Gas mark 7. Makes 2 pizza bases. **Serves** 2.

## Pitta bread pizzas

*2 wholewheat pitta breads*
*90ml/ 6 tbsp tomato sauce (see page 12)*
*175g/ 6 oz ricotta, cottage or low fat curd cheese*
*15ml/ 1 tbsp parsley or chives, chopped*
*125g/ 4 oz ham or chicken, chopped*
*125g/ 4 oz mild cheese, grated*

### Method
Place the pitta breads on a baking sheet and spread with tomato sauce. Cover with the ricotta cheese and sprinkle with the herbs. Arrange the ham or chicken on top and cover with the mild cheese. Place under a hot grill for about 10 minutes until bubbling and golden brown (or cook in a hot oven). You can also make pizzas using halved wholemeal muffins, crumpets or soda bread. **Serves** 2.

## Pizza toppings

### Pepperoni and chilli pizza
*90ml/ 6 tbsp tomato sauce (page 12)*
*125g/ 4 oz mushrooms, chopped*
*1 onion, chopped*
*250g/ 8 oz Mozzarella or other semi-soft cheese, grated*
*175g/ 6 oz Pepperoni sausage, sliced*
*1 green chilli, deseeded and diced*
*8 black olives*
*sprinkling of dried oregano*

### Method
Spread 2 pizza bases with the tomato sauce,

*From left to right:* Pepperoni and chilli pizza; Tandoori chicken kebabs; Anchovy and vegetable pizza.

and sprinkle with the mushrooms, onion and cheese. Dot with the Pepperoni, chilli and olives. Sprinkle with oregano. Bake in a preheated oven, 220°C/425°F/Gas mark 7, for 15-20 minutes. **Serves** 2.

## Anchovy and vegetable pizza

*90ml/6 tbsp tomato sauce (page 12)*
*1 green pepper, sliced*
*4 tomatoes, sliced*
*1 small courgette, diced*
*250g/8 oz Mozzarella or other semi-soft*
  *cheese, grated*
*95g/3½ oz can tuna, drained*
*1 can anchovy fillets, drained*
*8 stuffed olives, sliced*
*sprinkling of mixed herbs*

### Method

Spread 2 pizza bases with the tomato sauce. Cover with the green pepper, tomato and courgette. Sprinkle with the cheese and lay the tuna, anchovy fillets and olives on top. Sprinkle with the herbs, and bake in a pre-heated oven, 220°C/425°F/Gas mark 7, for 15-20 minutes. **Serves** 2.

## Tandoori chicken kebabs

*juice of ½ lemon*
*1 small onion, chopped*
*1 clove garlic, crushed*
*150ml/¼ pint natural yoghurt*
*1ml/good pinch of ground coriander*
*1ml/good pinch of ground cumin*
*5ml/1 tsp tandoori spice mix*
*salt and pepper*
*500g/1 lb chicken breasts, skinned and*
  *boned*

### Method

Blend the lemon juice, onion and garlic to a smooth paste in a liquidizer. Mix with the yoghurt, coriander, cumin, tandoori mix and seasoning. Cut the chicken into cubes and place in a Tupperware bowl. Cover with the yoghurt mixture. Seal and refrigerate for a few hours.

Thread the chicken onto skewers and cook under a hot grill for about 10 minutes, turning occasionally. Serve with rice cooked in the Multi Server, and salad. **Serves** 2.

## Cooking pasta in a Multi Server

### Dried pasta

Place 250g/8 oz (approximately) dried pasta in the colander of the Multi Server. Pour over just enough boiling water to barely cover the pasta. Add a pinch of salt and stir. Cover and leave for 15-20 minutes. Drain and use as required.

### Fresh pasta

Place 250g/8 oz (approximately) fresh pasta in the colander. Pour over hot water and add a pinch of salt. Stir and cover for 3-5 minutes depending on the type of pasta. Drain and use as required. Just toss in a little melted butter, chopped parsley and black pepper.

## Pasta and vegetable supper

*1 cauliflower*
*2 courgettes, sliced*
*½ cabbage, shredded*
*175g/6 oz pasta shapes, wholemeal or white*

Mushroom sauce:
*125g/4 oz button mushrooms, diced*
*20g/¾ oz sunflower margarine*
*20g/¾ oz wholemeal flour*
*300ml/½ pint milk*
*salt and freshly ground black pepper*
*pinch of paprika pepper*
*125g/4 oz Mozzarella or Cheddar cheese*
*parsley to garnish*

### Method

Divide the cauliflower into small florets, and mix all the vegetables together. Place the vegetables on the base of a shallow oven-proof dish. Cook the pasta in a Tupperware Multi Server until just tender. Drain and mix in with the vegetables.

While the pasta is cooking, make the sauce. Soften the mushrooms in the margarine for a few minutes, gradually adding the flour. Then stir in the milk gradually, to make a smooth sauce. Bring to the boil, stirring all the time, to thicken. Season well with salt, black pepper and paprika.

When the pasta is cooked arrange in an even layer over the vegetables. Then pour the mushroom sauce over the pasta. Grate the cheese with a Chop-N-Grate and sprinkle on top of the dish. Bake in a pre-heated oven at 190°C/375°F/Gas mark 5 for 20 minutes, until golden brown. Sprinkle with parsley. **Serves** 4.

## Chilli con carne

*30ml/2 tbsp oil*
*2 onions, chopped*
*15-30ml/1-2 tbsp chilli seasoning*
*750g/1½ lb lean beef, minced*
*439g/15 oz can kidney beans*
*439g/15 oz can chopped tomatoes*
*142g/5 oz can tomato purée*
*30ml/2 tbsp Worcestershire sauce*
*5ml/1 tsp sugar*
*5ml/1 tsp vinegar*
*salt and pepper*

### Method

Heat the oil in a large pan, add the onions and cook for 5 minutes until soft and golden. Add the chilli seasoning and cook for 1 minute, then add the beef and brown well. Add the remaining ingredients, including the liquid from the canned beans and bring to simmering point.

Cover and cook in a preheated oven at 160°C/325°F/Gas mark 3, for 1 hour. **Serves** 4.

## Soaking bulgar wheat

Measure out the quantity of bulgar wheat that you need. For the salad below, use a Tupperware 250ml cup.

Place in a Multi Server and pour in sufficient cold water to cover. Cover with the lid and leave for 20 minutes. Drain and

*Right above:* Chilli con carne; *below:* Chicken and carrot burgers.

pour away the liquid.

Use in salads, soups, casseroles, pies and meat dishes to add fibre, and to extend the meat in recipes.

———————⌘———————

## Wheat and nut salad

*250ml cup/6 oz bulgar wheat, soaked and*
    *drained*
*4 spring onions, chopped*
*1 bunch watercress, chopped*
*grated rind and juice of 1 lemon*
*plenty of parsley, chopped*
*1 clove garlic, crushed*
*125g/4 oz walnuts, chopped*
*30ml/2 tbsp vinaigrette (see page 13)*
*watercress leaves to garnish*

### Method
Mix all the salad ingredients together in a Salad Bowl and garnish with watercress leaves.

## Chicken and carrot burgers

*3 skinless chicken breasts, cubed*
*1 large onion, chopped*
*3 medium carrots, chopped*
*3 sprigs of fresh parsley*
*100ml cup/3½ oz bulgar wheat, soaked*
*salt and freshly ground pepper*
*sunflower oil for brushing*

### Method
Place all the ingredients into a food processor and blend until smooth. Make into thick burgers using a Hamburger Press and Freezer Set. Use straight away or freeze.

Thaw before cooking if frozen. Brush with a little sunflower oil, place under a medium grill and cook for about 15-20 minutes, turning once. Serve with baked potatoes, tomato sauce (see page 12) and salad. **Serves** 3-4.

**To freeze:** Stack in containers, seal, label and freeze.

## Summer wheel salad

### Tomato and cucumber salad
*½ cucumber, sliced*
*3 tomatoes, sliced*
*15ml/1 tbsp chives, chopped*
*15ml/1 tbsp vinaigrette (see page 13)*

#### Method
Arrange the cucumber and tomatoes in a section of the Party Server and sprinkle with chives and the dressing.

### Apple cabbage salad
*¼ white cabbage, shredded*
*1 red apple, diced*
*25g/1 oz walnuts, chopped*
*1 spring onion, chopped*
*30ml/2 tbsp mayonnaise (see page 13)*
*freshly ground black pepper*

#### Method
Mix all the salad ingredients together and arrange in the Party Server.

### Beetroot and carrot salad
*2 beetroots, cooked, sliced or diced*
*3 carrots, grated*
*1 orange, peeled*
*30ml/2 tbsp orange dressing (see page 13)*

#### Method
Arrange the beetroot, carrot and orange cut into skinless segments in the Party Server. Spoon over the dressing and sprinkle with black pepper.

### French bean and chicken salad
*125g/4 oz French or runner beans*
*175g/6 oz cooked chicken, cut in strips*
*2 hard-boiled eggs, chopped*
*30ml/2 tbsp yoghurt and mint dressing (see page 13)*

#### Method
Trim the beans and cook for 5 minutes until just soft. Cool in running water. Arrange the beans and chicken in the Party Server, sprinkle with the egg and spoon over the dressing.

#### To complete
Fill the centre of the Party Server with watercress or lettuce. Cover and refrigerate until needed. **Serves** 6.

## Courgette and carrot quick- fry

*15ml/1 tbsp olive oil*
*2 carrots, finely grated*
*2 courgettes, finely grated*
*15ml/1 tbsp parsley, chopped*

#### Method
Heat the olive oil for a few minutes, add the vegetables and cook quickly for about 1-2 minutes, stirring frequently.

Serve in little piles on each individual serving plate and sprinkle with parsley. **Serves** 4.

# Vegetarian stir-fry

3 spring onions, sliced diagonally
8 cauliflower florets
8 broccoli florets
2 courgettes, cut into strips
1 red pepper, cut into strips
3 sticks of celery, cut into strips
2 carrots, cut into strips
75ml/5 tbsp sunflower oil
1 clove garlic, crushed
30ml/2 tbsp oyster sauce
salt and freshly ground black pepper
nuts, sultanas and curry spices to garnish

## Method

Prepare all the vegetables in advance. Store in Tupperware bowls in the refrigerator until ready to cook.

Heat the oil in a large deep-sided frying pan or wok. Add the vegetables and garlic and stir occasionally, cooking for about 5 minutes. Stir in the oyster sauce to coat the vegetables and season.

Serve immediately with brown rice (see page 24), garnished with nuts, sultanas and a pinch of curry spices.
**Serves** 4.

# Mixed bean salad

397g/14 oz can red kidney beans
397g/14 oz can flageolet beans
397g/14 oz can chick peas
2 spring onions, sliced
125g/4 oz French beans, halved and cooked
30ml/2 tbsp parsley, chopped
60ml/4 tbsp vinaigrette dressing (see page 13)
salt and freshly ground black pepper

## Method

Drain and rinse the canned beans and chick peas under cold running water. Mix in a Space Saver Bowl with the remaining ingredients. Season well, cover and refrigerate until required. **Serves** 4.

*Left to right:* Summer wheel salad with, *(clockwise from the top):* tomato and cucumber salad, French bean and chicken salad, beetroot and carrot salad, apple cabbage salad; Courgette and carrot quick-fry; Mixed bean salad.

# Cooking cauliflower in the Multi Server

**1** Trim the cauliflower and cut into florets. Place in the colander of the Multi Server and rinse under cold running water. Drain. Place the cauliflower in a saucepan of hot water, bring to the boil, cook for 3-5 minutes and then pour into the Multi Server colander in the bowl. Cover and leave for 10 minutes. If you prefer a more crunchy texture, place the colander and cauliflower in the Multi Server. Pour over enough boiling water to cover the cauliflower. Cover and leave for 14-20 minutes.

**2** Lift the colander from the Multi Server and allow to drain.

## Cauliflower au gratin

1 cauliflower
1 quantity of béchamel sauce (see page 12)
175g/6 oz Cheddar cheese, grated
125g/4 oz wholewheat breadcrumbs

**Method**
Cook the cauliflower as above. Place in an ovenproof dish and pour over the béchamel sauce. Top with the cheese and breadcrumbs. Bake in a preheated oven at 200°C/400°F/Gas mark 6 for 10-15 minutes. **Serves** 2-4.

## Cauliflower and fruit salad

1 cauliflower, cut into florets
75g/3 oz chopped dates
1 banana, sliced
¼ cucumber, sliced
150ml/¼ pint lemon mayonnaise (see page 13)
15ml/1 tbsp parsley, chopped
freshly ground black pepper

**Method**
Cook the cauliflower in the Multi Server. Drain and rinse under cold water. Combine all the ingredients in a salad Serving Bowl. Serve with a green salad and crusty granary bread. **Serves** 4-6.

# Rogan vegetable curry

*Above:* Rogan vegetable curry

*2 onions, sliced*
*30ml/2 tbsp sunflower oil*
*15ml/1 tbsp tomato purée*
*45g/1.6 oz sachet Rogan Josh curry sauce*
  *mix*
*2 potatoes, cut in quarters*
*2 carrots, sliced*
*1 swede, diced*
*30ml/2 tbsp chutney*
*450ml/¾ pint water*
*1 cauliflower, cut into florets*
*125g/4 oz peas*
*15ml/1 tbsp desiccated coconut*

## Method

Fry the onion in the oil in a heavy-based saucepan. Add the tomato purée and Rogan Josh. Stir and cook for 5 minutes. Add all the prepared vegetables, except the cauliflower and peas. Stir in the chutney and water to cover. Simmer for 30 minutes until the vegetables are tender.

Add the cauliflower and peas, and continue cooking for 10 minutes. Add a little more water if necessary. Serve with rice (see page 24) and side dishes such as cucumber and yoghurt, pappadums and chutneys. **Serves** 2.

# Cranberry jelly mould

*2 packets of raspberry jelly*
*4 small jars of cranberry sauce*
*dash of wine vinegar*
*squeeze of lemon juice*
*125g/ 4 oz peeled prawns*
*30ml/ 2 tbsp mayonnaise*
*15ml/ 1 tbsp natural yoghurt*
*chicory leaves and fresh watercress to garnish*

## Method
Make up the jelly according to the instructions. While it is cooling whisk in the cranberry sauce and vinegar. Pour into a 1.5 litre Jel-Ring and cover with the seal. Refrigerate until set.

To serve, remove the seal and cover with a Serve-It-All plate. Invert the jelly on to the plate. Remove the centre seal and lift off the mould. Combine the mayonnaise, yoghurt and lemon juice, and toss the prawns in the mixture. Arrange the chicory in the centre of the jelly and fill with the prawns. Garnish with water-cress. **Serves** 6-8.

# Cucumber chartreuse

*300g/ 10 oz lime jelly tablets*
*900ml/ 1½ pints hot water*
*300ml/ ½ pint cider vinegar*
*15ml/ 1 tbsp caster sugar*
*few drops green vegetable colouring*
*500g/ 1 lb cucumber, peeled and diced*
*mustard and cress and sliced tomato to*
*garnish*

## Method
Separate the lime jelly into cubes and place in a Mix-N-Stor. Pour in the hot water and stir to dissolve the jelly. Add the vinegar, sugar and food colouring. Leave to cool until the consistency of unbeaten egg white.

Fold in the cucumber and when evenly suspended throughout the jelly pour into a 1.5 litre Jel-Ring. Cover with the seal and refrigerate until set. Remove the seal, invert a Serve-It-All Plate onto the jelly and turn over. Remove the centre and then lift off the mould. Fill the centre with tomatoes and cress. **Serves** 6.

# Vegetable fish terrine

*500g/ 1 lb haddock fillet*
*1 onion, roughly chopped*
*1 carrot, roughly chopped*
*juice of 1 lemon*
*300ml/ ½ pint double cream*
*10ml/ 2 tsp horseradish sauce*
*salt and freshly ground black pepper*
*30ml/ 2 tbsp parsley, chopped*
*15g/ ½ oz gelatine*
*2 egg whites, size 3*
*2 courgettes, cooked and puréed*
*2 carrots, cooked and puréed*
*250g/ 8 oz smoked salmon*
*2 smoked trout fillets*

## Method
Cook the haddock in a Multi Server with the onion, carrot and lemon juice in the base of the dish (see page 32). Lift out the fillet, remove the skin and flake the fish. Purée in a food processor and then gradually add the cream through the feed funnel. Add the horseradish, seasoning and parsley.

Dissolve the gelatine in 75ml/4 fl oz boiling water according to the packet instructions. Add half of the gelatine slowly to the haddock mixture and turn into a large Multi Mixing Bowl. Whisk the egg whites until they form soft peaks and fold into the fish mixture. Divide the remaining gelatine between the courgette and carrot mixtures and stir well. Lay half the smoked salmon slices on the base of the

*Above:* Vegetable fish terrine.

seal of a Buffet Server. Smooth half the haddock mixture over the salmon, followed by the carrot purée. Lay the smoked trout on top, cover with the courgette purée and then the remaining creamed haddock. Finish with a layer of smoked salmon. Cover with the base and refrigerate for several hours.

To serve, invert so that the terrine is resting on the base, and remove the seal.

Trim the edges before serving. The terrine is suitable as a starter with a selection of salads and wholemeal bread. **Serves** 8-10.

**To freeze:** Once covered allow to cool completely. Label and freeze for up to one month.

## Mozzarella and salami salad

*500g/ 1 lb large ripe tomatoes*
*2 Mozzarella cheeses*
*125g/ 4 oz piece salami*
*8 anchovy fillets*
*8 black olives*
*75ml/ 3 fl oz vinaigrette (see page 13)*
*sprig fresh basil leaves*

### Method
Quarter the tomatoes and cut the quarters in half again. Cut the Mozzarella into large cubes. Mix the tomato and cheese with the salami, anchovies and olives in a Salad Server. Toss in the dressing and garnish with the basil leaves. **Serves** 4.

*Below:* Winter spinach salad.

## Winter spinach salad

*350g/ 12 oz spinach, trimmed*
*500g/ 1 lb peeled prawns*
*50g/ 2 oz toasted hazelnuts, roughly chopped*
*8 lychees, peeled and stoned*
*1 pomegranate, quartered*
*120ml/ 4 fl oz vinaigrette (see page 13)*
*30ml/ 2 tbsp parsley, chopped*

### Method
Wash and dry the spinach. Arrange in a Salad Server with the prawns, nuts and lychees. Carefully remove the bright red seeds from the pomegranate and add to the salad. Toss gently in the vinaigrette dressing and sprinkle some chopped parsley over the top. **Serves** 4.

## Hot dill potato salad

*500g/1 lb small or new potatoes*
*3 spring onions, chopped*
*10ml/2 tsp dried dill*
*few anchovy fillets*
*75ml/3 fl oz natural yoghurt* **or**
*    soured cream*
*squeeze lemon juice*
*salt and pepper*
*chopped dill or chives to garnish*

### Method
Boil the potatoes until tender but still firm. Cut into chunks and place in a Multi Server without the colander. Mix with the onion, dill and anchovies. Toss gently in the yoghurt and lemon juice. Season and sprinkle with herbs. Cover and serve the salad while it is still warm. **Serves** 4.

*Above:* Crunchy apple and cauliflower salad.

## Crunchy apple and cauliflower salad

*1 small cauliflower, in florets*
*3 sticks celery, chopped*
*2 small red dessert apples, diced*
*125g/4 oz peanuts*
*150ml/¼ pint natural yoghurt*
*juice of 1 orange*
*30ml/2 tbsp parsley, chopped*

### Method
Mix the cauliflower, celery, apple and peanuts together in a Salad Server. Blend the yoghurt and orange juice in a Quick Shake and pour onto the salad. Toss the salad gently and sprinkle with parsley. **Serves** 4.

## Walnut torte

*125g/ 4 oz soft brown sugar*
*4 egg yolks, size 3*
*150g/ 5 oz ground toasted walnuts*
*15ml/ 1 tbsp white breadcrumbs*
*3 egg whites*

Icing:
*25g/ 1 oz butter*
*15ml/ 1 tbsp maple or golden syrup*
*50g/ 2 oz soft brown sugar*
*300ml/ ½ pint double cream*
*walnut halves for decoration*

### Method

Place the sugar and egg yolks in a Multi Mixing Bowl fitted with the rim shield.

*From left to right:* Walnut torte; Profiteroles with hazelnut cream and chocolate sauce.

Whisk with an electric hand mixer until billowy. Fold in the walnuts and bread-crumbs. Whisk the egg whites in another bowl until stiff and fold into the mixture. Bake in a 20cm/8in flan tin in a preheated oven at 180°C/350°F/Gas mark 4 for 25 minutes. Cool and turn out.

To make the icing, melt the butter, syrup and sugar together. Stir in 60ml/4 tbsp of cream and bring to the boil. Cool, stirring occasionally. Whip the remaining cream in a Multi Mixing Bowl until stiff and fold into the syrup mixture.

Place the cake on a Domed Server with a pedestal. Smooth a layer of icing over the top of the cake. Using a piping bag with a star nozzle pipe the remaining icing into rosettes around the edge and in the centre of the cake. Decorate with walnut halves, as shown. **Serves** 6.

# Profiteroles with hazelnut cream and chocolate sauce

*150ml/¼ pint water*
*50g/2 oz butter or sunflower margarine*
*65g/2½ oz plain flour*
*2 eggs, size 3, beaten*

Filling:
*300ml/½ pint double cream*
*50g/2 oz hazelnuts, finely chopped*

Chocolate sauce:
*250ml cup/6 oz chocolate drops*
*10ml/2 tsp golden syrup*
*15g/½ oz butter*
*30ml/2 tbsp water*
*2.5ml/½ tsp vanilla essence*

## Method

Place the water and butter in a pan and bring to the boil. Remove from the heat and stir in the flour immediately. Beat until the mixture forms a ball and leaves the sides of the pan clean. Do not over-beat. When the mixture is cool, beat in the eggs, a little at a time, until you have a stiff glossy paste. Place in a piping bag with a plain nozzle and pipe into balls on a damp baking sheet. Bake about 10 at a time in a pre-heated oven at 200°C/400°F/Gas mark 6 for about 15-20 minutes until crisp and firm. Remove and cool. Cut a slit in each one to allow the steam to escape.

Beat the cream until stiff and add the hazelnuts. Use to fill the profiteroles. Melt all the sauce ingredients. Pile the profiteroles onto a Serve-It-All with a pedestal, and drizzle over the chocolate sauce. **Serves** 6.

## Cook's tip

To melt chocolate in the Multi Server, break into squares in a small bowl and place in the Multi Server. Pour about 600ml/1 pint boiling water into the Multi Server and cover for 10-15 minutes. The chocolate will melt gently.

# Fruit charlotte

## Fruit charlotte

*300ml/½ pint double cream*
*50g/2 oz caster sugar*
*100ml/3 fl oz boiling water*
*50ml/1½ fl oz orange juice*
*24 boudoir biscuits*
*450ml/¾ pint of fresh fruit, such as*
  *raspberries, strawberries, sliced peaches or*
  *plums,* **or** *thawed frozen fruit*

### Method

Place the cream in a Multi Mixing Bowl and whisk until thick. Dissolve the sugar in a Tupperware container with the boiling water and stir in the orange juice.

**1**  Place a design seal in the Tupperware Jel-N-Serve.

**2**  Dip the biscuits very quickly into the orange syrup and arrange around the edge of the Jel-N-Serve, fitting them into the curves.

**3**  Fill with some of the fruit and half the cream, then top with 4 biscuits. Add more fruit and the remaining cream, and cover with 4 biscuits.

**4**  Cover with the seal.

**5**  Press down firmly about 12 times to distribute the cream evenly. Refrigerate for several hours until set.

**6**  To serve, remove the large seal. Invert the serving tray over the mould and turn up the right way. Very carefully remove the design seal, and lift off the mould.

**7**  Decorate with piped cream and segments of fruit. Serve immediately.
**Serves** 4-6.

53

## Strawberry brandysnap gâteau

*6 eggs, size 3*
*30ml/ 2 tbsp hot water*
*175g/ 6 oz caster sugar*
*150g/ 5 oz plain flour*
*25g/ 1 oz cornflour*
*50g/ 2 oz butter, melted*

Syrup:
*50g/ 2 oz caster sugar*
*30ml/ 2 tbsp blackcurrant juice*
*10ml/ 2 tsp Grand Marnier*

Filling:
*450ml/ ¾ pint double cream, stiffly whipped*
*350g/ 12 oz fresh strawberries, hulled*
*50g/ 2 oz almonds, toasted and chopped*
*8-10 brandy snap curls*

### Method
Grease and line two 20cm/8in round cake tins. Whisk the eggs, water and sugar together in a bowl over a pan of hot water, or use a large food mixer. Whisk until the mixture becomes very thick and pale, and leaves a trail with a spoon. This can take at least 5-10 minutes. Sift the flour and cornflour together, and gently fold into the egg mixture. Then fold in the butter. Scoop into the tins with a Paddle Scraper. Bake in a preheated oven at 190°C/375°F/Gas mark 5 for 20-25 minutes. Cool slightly.

Melt the sugar, blackcurrant juice and Grand Marnier together, bring to the boil and reduce by half. Brush over the sponges carefully. Sandwich the sponges together, with some of the cream and strawberries between, and place on the base of a Domed Server. Spread half the remaining cream over the top and sides of the cake. Press the almonds onto the sides.

Arrange the brandysnaps as illustrated. Pipe the remaining cream into rosettes between the brandysnaps and around the edge. Decorate with the remaining straw-

berries. Store covered in the Domed Server. **Serves** 8-10.

**To freeze:** Freeze in the Domed Server without the brandysnaps. Label and freeze for up to 1 month.

## Piano pavlova

*3 egg whites, size 3*
*45ml/3 tbsp hot water*
*5ml/1 tsp cornflour*
*175g/6 oz caster sugar*
*5ml/1 tsp vinegar*
*5ml/1 tsp vanilla essence*

Topping:
*120ml/4 fl oz double cream*
*120ml/4 fl oz fromage frais*
*2 kiwi fruit, sliced*
*1 banana, sliced*
*125g/4 oz seedless black grapes*

*Above left:* Strawberry brandysnap gâteau; *above right:* Piano pavlova.

**Method**
Measure a circle slightly smaller than the base of a Domed Server on a sheet of waxed baking parchment. Place this circle on a baking sheet. Whisk the egg whites and hot water in a food mixer or with a hand mixer for 1 minute. Add the cornflour and sugar and whip for 15 minutes. Add the vinegar and vanilla essence. Spread the meringue onto the circle on the baking tray. Bake in a preheated oven at 200°C/400°F/Gas mark 6 for 2 minutes. Turn off the heat and leave for one hour. Remove from the oven, place a Domed Server plate on top and turn over. Peel off the paper. Cover and cool. (The meringue will keep for up to a week sealed in a Tupperware Domed Server.)

Whip the cream and fold in the fromage frais. Spread over the meringue and decorate with the fresh fruit. **Serves** 6.

# Basic scone mixture

*250g/8 oz white or wholemeal self-raising*
  *flour*
*2.5ml/½ tsp salt*
*5ml/1 tsp baking powder*
*50g/2 oz butter or sunflower margarine*
*150ml/¼ pint milk*
*milk to glaze*

## Method

Mix the flour, salt and baking powder in a Multi Mixing Bowl. Rub in the butter until the mixture resembles fine breadcrumbs. Stir in enough milk to give a soft dough.

Roll out on a floured Pastry Sheet. Cut into rounds with the Cookie Cutter Set and place on a greased baking tray. Brush the tops with a little milk and bake in a pre-heated oven at 220°C/425°F/Gas mark 7 for 8-10 minutes. Cool and serve immediately, split in half, with butter. **Makes** 10-12 scones.

**To freeze:** When cool place in a Freeze-N-Stor, seal, label and freeze.

## Variations

### Fruit scones:

*add 50g/2 oz sultanas or raisins and a pinch of mixed spice.*

### Date scones:

*add 50g/2 oz chopped dates and 15ml/1 tbsp brown sugar.*

### Rich tea scones:

*add 15ml/1 tbsp caster sugar, 1 egg, size 2, beaten and 50g/2 oz glacé cherries, rinsed and chopped.*

### Wholemeal cheese scones:

*(using wholemeal self-raising flour): add 75g/3 oz Cheddar cheese, grated, 5ml/1 tsp paprika pepper and a pinch of salt.*

*From left to right:* Scones; Wholemeal chocolate cookies; Spicy carrot cake.

# Spicy carrot cake

350g/12 oz carrots, grated
4 eggs, size 3
250g/8 oz brown sugar
175ml/6 fl oz sunflower oil
250g/8 oz wholemeal self-raising flour
5ml/1 tsp cinnamon
10ml/2 tsp mixed spice
125g/4 oz desiccated coconut
125g/4 oz sultanas or raisins

Topping:
125g/4 oz low-fat soft cheese
grated rind and juice of 1 lemon
15ml/1 tbsp caster sugar
25g/1 oz desiccated coconut, toasted

## Method

Grate the carrots with the Chop-N-Grate. Whisk the eggs and sugar together until thick and billowy in a Multi Mixing Bowl fitted with the rim seal. Whisk in the oil. Fold in the remaining ingredients. Divide between 2 18-20cm/7-8in cake tins. Smooth the tops and bake in a preheated oven at 190°C/375°F/Gas mark 5 for 20-25 minutes. Cool. Freeze one cake for future use.

To make the topping mix the cheese, lemon and sugar together and spread over the cake. Sprinkle with coconut. Serve or store in a Serve-It-All plate and cover. **Serves** 6-8 per cake.

**To freeze:** Place the cake minus the topping in a Freeze-N-Stor. Seal, label and freeze. Store for 1 month. Defrost, make up the topping and spread over the cake. The icing can be made up in advance and frozen separately.

---

# Wholemeal chocolate cookies

350g/12 oz sunflower margarine
500g/1 lb wholemeal self-raising flour
250g/8 oz brown sugar
pinch salt
150g/5 oz chocolate drops
2 eggs, size 3

## Method

Place the margarine and flour in a Multi Mixing Bowl. Rub in the margarine until the mixture resembles breadcrumbs. Add the sugar, salt and chocolate drops. Mix in the eggs to make a soft dough. Roll out on a lightly floured Pastry Sheet until about 0.5-1cm/¼-½inch thick. Cut into rounds and shapes using the Cookie Cutter Set. Place on a greased baking tray and bake in a preheated oven at 180°C/350°F/Gas mark 4 for 12 minutes until golden. Leave for a few minutes on the tray and then cool in a wire rack. Store in a Cookie Jar (Ultra Clear Collection). **Makes** 25-30 cookies.

# Raspberry Swiss roll

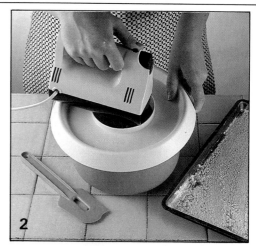

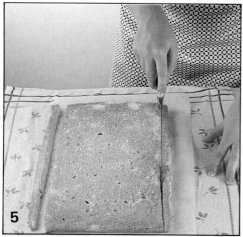

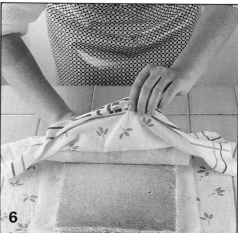

*50g/ 2 oz soft margarine*
*125ml/ 4 fl oz caster sugar*
*2 eggs, size 2*
*2ml/ ½ tsp vanilla essence*
*pinch of salt*
*200ml cup/ 4 oz self-raising flour, sieved*
*150ml/ ¼ pint double cream*
*125g/ 4 oz fresh raspberries*

## Method

**1** Place the margarine, sugar, eggs, vanilla and half the flour in a Multi Mixing Bowl.

**2** Fit the shield seal to the Bowl and beat with an electric hand mixer until creamy. Fold in the remaining flour and the salt.

**3** Pour the mixture into a greased and floured Swiss roll tin and smooth over. Bake in a preheated oven at 200°C/ 400°F/Gas mark 6 for 10 minutes, until firm to the touch.

**4** Meanwhile, lay a damp tea towel on the work surface. Cover with a large sheet of greaseproof paper and sprinkle with caster sugar.

**5** Turn the cake out immediately onto the paper. Quickly trim the edges.

**6** Gently and quickly roll up the cake from the short end, letting the paper roll up inside. Wrap in the cloth and leave to cool. When cool, unroll the cake carefully.

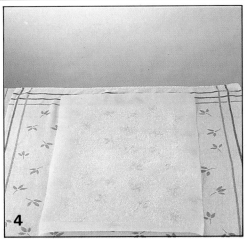

**7** Whip the cream until softly stiff and spread evenly over the cake. Dot the raspberries over the cream, reserving a few for decoration and re-roll the cake.

**8** Sprinkle with caster sugar, decorate with raspberries and serve on the Buffet Server. **Serves** 6-8.

### Filling variations

### Lemon cheese filling

*30ml/2 tbsp lemon curd*
*300ml/½ pint double cream, whipped*
*grated rind of 1 lemon*
*1 lemon, sliced for decoration*
*25g/1 oz pistachio nuts or toasted almonds*

**Method**
Spread the cooled, unrolled sponge with lemon curd. Add the lemon rind to the whipped cream, and spread over the lemon curd. Roll the cake up. Pipe the remaining cream into rosettes on top of the cake, decorate with lemon slices and pistachio nuts. Alternatively, use fromage frais or crème fraîche instead of cream.

### Raspberry dessert

Spread the sponge with fromage frais and raspberries. Serve sliced, with puréed fresh raspberries with a little added sugar.

# Banana cake

*50g/2 oz sunflower margarine*
*175g/6 oz light soft brown sugar*
*175g/6 oz natural yoghurt*
*2 eggs, size 2*
*275g/9 oz wholemeal self-raising flour*
*2 bananas, mashed*
*125g/4 oz sultanas*
*5ml/1 tsp mixed spice*

## Method

Place the margarine and sugar in a Multi Mixing Bowl. Beat in the remaining ingredients. Spoon into a greased 20cm/8in cake tin and bake in a preheated oven at 180°C/350°F/Gas mark 4 for 1¼-1½ hours. Cool in the tin and turn out onto a wire tray. **Serves** 8.

**To freeze:** Place in a Domed Server, label and freeze.

# Welsh tea bread

*300g/10 oz mixed dried fruit*
*150g/5 oz brown sugar (Barbados)*
*grated rind of 1 lemon*
*300ml/½ pint strong tea*
*350g/12 oz wholemeal self-raising flour*
*10ml/2 tsp mixed spice*
*5ml/1 tsp cinnamon*
*1 egg, size 3*

## Method

Mix the fruit, sugar, lemon rind and tea in a 2 litre Mix-N-Stor. Cover and leave overnight. Strain the fruit, reserving the liquid.

Mix the fruit into the remaining ingredients with enough liquid to give a soft dropping consistency. Place in a greased 1kg/2lb loaf tin and bake in a pre-heated oven at 180°C/350°F/Gas mark 4 for 50 minutes. The cake should be firm to the touch when cooked. Cool and serve sliced and buttered. **Serves** 6-8.

# Apple buns

*250g/8 oz wholemeal self-raising flour*
*pinch of salt*
*5ml/1 tsp mixed spice*
*175g/6 oz sunflower margarine*
*75g/3 oz brown sugar*
*250g/8 oz cooking apples, diced*
*1 egg, beaten*

## Method

Mix the flour, salt and spice together in a Multi Mixing Bowl. Rub in the margarine and stir in the apple and egg. Place heaped spoonfuls on a greased baking tray, leaving space between each. Bake in a preheated oven at 190°C/375°F/Gas mark 5 for 20 minutes. Cool a little and serve warm. **Serves** 8-12.

# Quick processor granary and walnut bread

*625g/1¼ lb granary flour*
*10ml/2 tsp salt*
*1 sachet easy-blend yeast*
*30ml/2 tbsp sunflower oil*
*300ml/½ pint warm water*
*30ml/2 tbsp molasses*
*60ml/4 tbsp cracked wheat*
*125g/4 oz walnuts, chopped*
*beaten egg to glaze*

## Method

Using a plastic dough blade, mix the flour, salt and yeast in the food processor for a few seconds at high speed. While the machine is operating, pour in the oil, water and molasses through the feeder tube. Then add the cracked wheat and walnuts. Process for about 1 minute until the mixture is smooth and leaves the side of the bowl clean. Remove the dough and place in a Fix-N-Mix bowl. Seal and leave in a warm place until the dough has doubled its size and the seal 'pops'.

Turn out onto a lightly floured Pastry

Sheet. Knead lightly to knock back any large air bubbles and thereby give an even texture to the bread. Shape into two loaves and brush the tops with beaten egg.

Place on a greased baking sheet and leave in a warm place – until the loaves reach the required size (about 25-30 minutes). When risen, bake in a preheated oven at 220°C/425°F/Gas mark 7 for 25-35 minutes. To test if the bread is cooked,

*Clockwise from the top:* Quick processor granary and walnut bread; Apple buns; Banana cake.

remove from the oven and tap the base of the loaf with your knuckles. If it sounds hollow, it is cooked. Allow to cool. **Makes 2 loaves.**

**To freeze:** Cool thoroughly and place in a Freeze-N-Stor. Seal, label and freeze.

## Granola

*3 x 250ml cups/ 10 oz jumbo oats*
*1 x 150ml cup/ 2 oz bran*
*1 x 100ml cup/ 1 oz wheatgerm*
*1 x 100ml cup/ 2 oz hazelnuts, chopped*
*1 x 250ml cup/ 4 oz desiccated coconut*
*2.5ml/ ½ tsp salt*
*1 x 100ml cup/ 2 oz sesame seeds*
*125ml/ 4 fl oz sunflower oil*
*125ml/ 4 fl oz clear honey*
*few drops of vanilla essence*
*1 x 200ml cup/ 5 oz stoned raisins*
*1 x 100ml cup/ 2 oz chopped Brazil nuts*
*1 x 50ml cup/ 1 oz chopped cashew nuts*

### Method

Mix the oats, bran, wheatgerm, hazelnuts, cocount, salt and sesame seeds together. Heat the oil and honey gently until blended. Add the vanilla and pour over the granola mixture and coat well. Spread over the base of a baking tin and bake in a pre-heated oven at 140°C/275°F/Gas mark 1 for 35-40 minutes. Turn occasionally. Cool and stir in the raisins, brazil and cashew nuts.

Store in a Space Saver. **Makes** about 1kg/2lbs of the mixture.

## Kedgeree

*250g/ 8 oz smoked haddock fillets*
*250ml cup/ 8 oz white or Easy-Cook*
  *brown rice*
*1 large onion, chopped*
*50g/ 2 oz butter or sunflower margarine*
*10ml/ 2 tsp paprika pepper*
*pinch of chilli powder*
*30ml/ 2 tbsp parsley, chopped*
*grated rind and juice of 1 lemon*
*25g-50g/ 1-2 oz butter*
*125g/ 4 oz frozen peas*

To garnish:
*4 eggs, lightly boiled (5-6 minutes) and*
  *quartered*
*sprinkling of paprika and parsley*

### Method

Loosely roll up the smoked haddock fillets and cook in a Multi Server (see page 30) for 20 minutes. Remove and flake. Cook the rice in the Multi Server (see page 24). Sauté the onion in the butter in a frying pan. Add

the rice, haddock and remaining ingredients. Stir constantly to heat through and avoid sticking. To serve turn into the Multi Server with 300ml/½ pint hot water in the base to keep the dish hot. Garnish with eggs and parsley. **Serves** 4.

## Home-made muesli

*4 x 250ml cups/ 12 oz jumbo oats*
*1 x 200ml cup/ 3 oz rye flakes*
*1 x 150ml cup/ 2 oz bran*
*1 x 100ml cup/ 1 oz wheatgerm*
*1 x 150ml cup/ 4 oz raisins*
*1 x 150ml cup/ 4 oz chopped dates*
*1 x 100ml cup/ 2 oz hazelnuts*
*1 x 100ml cup/ 2 oz walnuts*
*1 x 50ml cup/ 1 oz cashew nuts*
*1 x 100ml cup/ 2 oz Brazil nuts*
*1 x 100ml cup/ 3 oz dried apricots, chopped*

### Method
Measure all the ingredients in a Mix-N-Stor. Seal and shake to mix well. Store in a Space Saver. Serve with milk or yoghurt. **Makes** approximately 1kg/2lb.

## Home-made yoghurt

*600ml/ 1 pint cow's milk*
*15ml/ 1 tbsp skimmed milk powder*
*60ml/ 4 tbsp natural live yoghurt*

### Method
Heat the milk to boiling point. Remove from the heat and cool to 43°C/110-112°F. (Use a sugar thermometer to get an accurate reading.) Mix the skimmed milk powder with the yoghurt 'starter'. Stir into the warmed milk and pour into three 200ml Space Saver Rounds. Seal. Place in the colander of a Multi Server with hot water so the pots are half-immersed. Cover and leave for at least 4 hours. Check that the yoghurt has set and refrigerate for at least 12 hours before eating.

**Note:** Clean the yoghurt containers thoroughly in boiling hot water. Live yoghurt can be bought from most health food stores. Most commercial yoghurts have been pasteurized killing the bacteria needed to make yoghurt.

*From left to right:* Granola; Muesli; Kedgeree; Yoghurt.

## Stuffed chicken breasts

*4 large chicken breasts, boned and skinned*
*8 rashers back bacon* **or**
*4 rashers middle cut bacon*

Stuffing:
*125g/ 4 oz wholewheat breadcrumbs*
*2 rashers streaky bacon, chopped*
*2 spring onions, chopped*
*15ml/ 1 tbsp dried tarragon*
*30ml/ 2 tbsp natural yoghurt*
*salt and freshly ground black pepper*

### Method
Slit the chicken breasts lengthways until partly open. Mix all the stuffing ingredients together in a Multi Mixing Bowl and use to fill the chicken breasts.

*From below centre to right:* Vegetable kebabs; Barbecue spare ribs; Stuffed chicken breasts.

Reshape and wrap each one in a bacon rasher. Secure with a cocktail stick. Place in a Serving Plate Set, cover and refrigerate, ready for transport to the barbecue. **Serves** 4.

To barbecue wrap the chicken pieces in foil and bake on a barbecue for 30 minutes. Carefully remove the foil and brown the outside on the barbecue for about 5-10 minutes.

In a conventional oven bake in a preheated oven at 180°C/350°F/Gas mark 4 for 45 minutes. **Serves** 4.

## Garlic bread

*1 French bread stick, white or wholemeal*
*175g/ 6 oz butter, softened*
*2 cloves garlic, crushed*
*30ml/ 2 tbsp parsley, chopped*
*grated rind of 1 lemon*

## Method

Cut slits across the bread without cutting right through. Beat the remaining ingredients together or blend in a food processor. Spread each side of each slit in the bread with the butter. Wrap in foil and cook over a barbecue. Alternatively, bake in a preheated oven at 200°C/400°F/Gas mark 6 for 15 minutes. Unwrap, cut and serve. **Serves** 6.

## Vegetable kebabs

*1 green pepper*
*1 red pepper*
*8-10 button mushrooms*
*2 onions*
*2 courgettes*

Dressing:
*30ml/ 2 tbsp olive oil*
*15ml/ 1 tbsp orange juice*
*30ml/ 2 tbsp lemon juice*
*60ml/ 4 tbsp mixed parsley, sage and basil,*
    *chopped*
*2 spring onions, chopped*

## Method

Cut the vegetables into largish chunks and thread on to 6 barbecue skewers. Place all the dressing ingredients in a Quick Shake container and shake a few times to mix.

Lay the kebabs on a Serving Plate without the colander tray, pour over the dressing, cover and refrigerate for one hour. Take to the barbecue, out of the Tupperware and cook until the vegetables just sizzle on the outside. **Serves** 6.

**Note:** Whole sweetcorn are also ideal for barbecues. Cut into wedges and thread on the skewers with the other vegetables.

## Barbecue spare ribs

*6-8 Chinese-style barbecue spare ribs*
Devilled sauce:
*15ml/ 1 tbsp dry mustard*
*5ml/ 1 tsp ground ginger*
*30ml/ 2 tbsp Hoi Sin barbecue sauce*
*15ml/ 1 tbsp thick honey*
*15ml/ 1 tbsp rich Soy sauce*

## Method

Lay the spare ribs in a rectangular Space Saver container. Mix all the sauce ingredients together and spread evenly over the spare ribs. Cover and refrigerate for 1 hour. Take to the barbecue in the Tupperware, remove from the container, and cook until richly brown all over, turning occasionally. **Serves** 4.

## Picnic ideas

Tupperware Carry Away and Picnic containers are the best choice for all those occasions when eating away from home.

All types of prepared and cooked meat dishes for barbecues can be transported in the Carry Away and taken to the fire in their individual pots to be cooked. In this way, food is kept covered for freshness and health.

Salads need not be made up. Separate ingredients can be layered in Tupperware containers along with other food and bread to allow the family to create their own dishes on the spot.

Pack breads and cakes in similar containers. Keep cooked meats and cheese in the refrigerator until the last minute before a picnic. This way food will stay as fresh as when it was made. On hot days, stack the Tupperware containers with ice packs on the meats and desserts.

*Below left:* Tuna and basil salad; *bottom left:* Chicken with tarragon and strawberries; Tupperware Carry Away containers and picnic ideas.

Young children like to have their own little picnic plates of food. Then they can go off and eat together.

Whole made-up salads are good for the more organized picnic when food does not have to travel too far. Prepare the salads and dressings separately and toss together just before eating.

School lunches are best prepared the night before. The whole box can be refrigerated for the next day.

Pack fruit such as grapes with a little tissue, or prepare the fruit and put in individual boxes, then everyone can help themselves.

## Chicken with tarragon and strawberries

*2 eggs, size 3*
*75ml/5 tbsp sugar*
*45ml/3 tbsp tarragon vinegar*
*150ml/¼ pint thick double cream*

5ml/1 tsp dried tarragon
salt and freshly ground black pepper
4 chicken breasts, cooked
125g/4 oz strawberries, hulled and sliced
1 bunch watercress, washed

## Method

Place the eggs and sugar into 2.0 litre Mix-N-Stor and place over a large pan of hot water. Using an electric whisk beat the mixture until very thick and creamy and leaves a trail. This can take a little while. Whisk the cream until thick. Gradually add the vinegar to the cream while continuing to whisk. Fold the egg mixture into the cream. Season to taste. This sauce can be stored in the Mix-N-Stor in the refrigerator for several days.

Remove the skin from the chicken and slice. Cut the cucumber into wedges. Arrange the chicken, cucumber and strawberries in a Square 1. Pour the dressing over the meat and lightly stir in the watercress leaves. Cover and chill until ready to serve. **Serves** 4.

## Tuna and basil salad

250g/8 oz pasta shapes, 3 colours
200g/7 oz tuna in oil, drained
1 red pepper, diced
1 green pepper, diced
¼ cucumber, diced
6 button mushrooms, sliced
4 spring onions, chopped
30ml/2 tbsp parsley, chopped
Dressing:
1 quantity of yoghurt and mint dressing
  (see page 12) using basil in place of mint
15ml/1 tbsp pesto sauce
1 clove garlic, crushed

## Method

Cook the pasta in boiling water for 10-12 minutes until just tender. Rinse under cold water, drain and place in a Salad Bowl. Add the tuna, peppers, cucumber, mushrooms, onions and parsley.

Make up the yoghurt dressing and stir in the pesto sauce and garlic. Pour over the pasta salad. Serve with garlic bread and plain lettuce. **Serves** 4.

## Chicken and pepper salad

*125g/ 4 oz cooked chicken, chopped*
*50g/ 2 oz pasta shells, cooked and drained*
*½ red pepper, diced*
*50g/ 2 oz cucumber, chopped*
*watercress leaves*

Dressing:
*30ml/ 2 tbsp natural yoghurt*
*15ml/ 1 tbsp mayonnaise*
*a few drops tomato purée*
*freshly ground black pepper and salt*
*pinch cayenne pepper*

### Method

Toss the chicken, pasta and salad ingredients together and place in a Snack Set. Shake all the dressing ingredients in a Quick Shake and pour into a Tupperware small round. Seal and pack with the salad. Coat the salad in the dressing just before serving. **Serves** 1 generous portion or 2 smaller ones.

Accompany the salad with wholemeal pitta bread, cos lettuce pieces or sticks of celery, wholemeal chocolate cookies (page 57), an apple, and a drink of your choice.

Chicken and pepper salad.

Sausages and baked bread rolls.

## Sausages and baked bread rolls

*500g/ 1 lb low-fat pork sausages*
*30ml/ 2 tbsp tomato relish*
*625ml/ 1¼ lb packet white bread mix*
*egg, size 3, to glaze*

### Method

Cook the sausages under a grill for about 5 minutes – just to brown. Place the bread mix in a Mix-N-Stor and make up according to the packet instructions. Roll the dough out on a Pastry Sheet and cut into 8 triangles. Place a sausage on each, spread with a little tomato relish and roll up to partially cover the sausage. Place on a greased baking sheet and glaze with beaten egg. Bake in a preheated oven at 200°C/ 400°F/Gas mark 6 for 15-20 minutes until brown. **Serves** 4.

**To freeze:** Interleave with greaseproof paper in a suitable Tupperware freezer container. Seal, label and freeze.

Accompany Sausage Bread Rolls with cucumber and carrots in a Snack Cup with a seal, a slice of Banana Cake (page 00), a small apple and apple juice to drink.

Beef turnovers.

## Beef turnovers

Pastry:
*350g/12 oz wholewheat flour*
*pinch of salt*
*175g/6 oz sunflower margarine*
*water to mix*
*egg to glaze*
Filling:
*175-250g/6-8 oz very lean braising steak,*
  *in chunks*
*2 carrots, chopped*
*1 onion, chopped*
*1 potato, chopped*
*salt and freshly ground black pepper*
*5ml/1 tsp tarragon*
*15ml/1 tbsp horseradish relish*
*10ml/2 tsp gravy granules*
*100ml/3½ fl oz boiling water*

### Method
Make the pastry as described on page 22. The dough should be fairly moist to enable easy handling. Roll out and cut into 6 14cm/5½in circles.

Mince the braising steak finely in a food processor. Set aside in a bowl. Process the vegetables finely and add to the meat. Season well and add the tarragon and horseradish. Dissolve the gravy granules in the water; once thickened, add to the meat and stir well. Divide the mixture between the pastry circles. Brush the edges with egg and fold the pastry over and seal. Glaze with the remaining egg. Bake in a pre-heated oven at 190°C/375°F/Gas mark 5 for 25-30 minutes. Reduce the oven temperature if the pastry is browning too quickly. Serve for a packed lunch or a quick snack. **Makes** 6.

**To freeze:** Pack when cool in a Freeze-N-Stor. Seal, label and freeze.

## Mushrooms in yoghurt dressing

*125g/4 oz button mushrooms*
Yoghurt dressing:
*125g/4 oz low-fat soft cheese*
*30ml/2 tbsp natural yoghurt*
*grated rind of 1 lemon*
*15ml/1 tbsp parsley, chopped*
*1 spring onion, finely chopped*
*salt and freshly ground black pepper*

### Method
Wipe the mushrooms dry after washing. Mix all the remaining ingredients in a Mix-N-Stor, and add the mushrooms. Spoon into one section of a Double Diner. Fill the other section with a salad and wholemeal bread roll. **Serves** 1-2.

Accompany Mushroom Salad with a little lean chicken in a wholewheat bap or slices of granary and walnut bread (page 60), a bunch of grapes and a drink of your choice.

Mushroom in yoghurt dressing.

## Quick yoghurt lollies

*300ml/½ pint milk*
*300g/flavoured set yoghurt*
*25ml/1½ tbsp caster sugar*

### Method
Place all the ingredients in a Multi Mixing Bowl. Put on the rim seal and whisk the ingredients together. Pour into 8 Ice Tups. Seal and freeze until firm. **Makes** 8 lollies.

### Variation
### Ribena and apple
*30ml/2 tbsp Ribena*
*600ml/1 pint apple juice*

### Method
Dilute the Ribena with the apple juice. Pour into 8 Ice Tups. Seal and freeze until firm.

## Baked potato varieties

### Cream cheese and bacon
*4 baking potatoes*

Filling:
*125g/4 oz low-fat soft cream cheese*
*4 rashers back bacon, cooked*
*15ml/1 tbsp parsley, chopped*
*freshly ground black pepper*

### Method
Scrub and prick the potatoes. Bake at 200°C/400°F/Gas mark 6 for approximately ¾-1 hour, depending on size. Split in half. Scoop out the potato and mix in a Multi Mixing Bowl with the cheese, bacon and parsley. Season to taste. Fill the potato shells and return to the oven for 10 minutes. **Serves** 4.

### Cheesy tomato
*4 baking potatoes*

Filling:
*30ml/2 tbsp tomato relish*
*125g/4 oz Edam cheese, grated*
*5ml/1 tsp mixed herbs*
*2 tomatoes, sliced*

### Method
Cook the potatoes as described above. Mix the relish, cheese and herbs with the cooked potato. Pile into the potato shells. Garnish with tomato slices and return to the oven for 10 minutes. **Serves** 4.

# Autumn supper

*250g/ 8 oz extra lean minced beef*
*15ml/ 1 tbsp sunflower oil*
*25ml/ 1½ tbsp tomato ketchup*
*250g/ 8 oz tomatoes, chopped*
*250g/ 8 oz button mushrooms, chopped*
*2.5ml/ ½ tsp dried tarragon*
*salt and freshly ground black pepper*
*25ml/ 1½ tbsp stock*
*300g/ 10 oz wholemeal pasta leaves*
*175g/ 6 oz cheese, grated*
*175g/ 6 oz carrot, grated*

## Method

Place the beef and oil in a saucepan and cook gently to brown the meat, turning with a fork. Stir in the tomato ketchup, tomatoes and mushrooms. Mix well and add the tarragon, seasoning and stock. Cover and simmer gently for 15 minutes. Cook the pasta with 750ml/ 1¼ pints of boiling salted water, simmer for 15 minutes until tender, or cook for 5 minutes and turn into a Tupperware Multi Server to finish cooking (see page 40). Serve the meat with the pasta and top with the cheese and carrot. **Serves** 4.

# Almond ice

*2 large cans evaporated milk*
*125g/ 4 oz ground almonds*
*175g/ 6 oz caster sugar*
*30ml/ 2 tbsp vanilla essence*
*50g/ 2 oz hazelnuts, chopped*
*1 chocolate flake bar, crumbled*

## Method

Place the milk, ground almonds, sugar and vanilla essence in a Multi Mixing Bowl. Fit the rim cover and whisk well. Cover with the centre seal and freeze until partially set. Fold in the hazelnuts and chocolate. Return to the freezer to set. Serve in scoops on crushed ice with a wafer.
**Serves** 6-8.

*From left to right:* Baked potato varieties; Quick yoghurt lollies; Autumn supper; Almond ice (with banana).

# Index

*Page numbers in italics refer to illustrations*

**A**
Almond ice                          71, *71*
Apple buns                          60. *61*
Apple cabbage salad                 42, *42*
Autumn supper                       70, *71*
Avocado                             19, *19*

**B**
Banana cake                         60, *61*
Barbecue spare ribs                 65, *65*
Béchamel sauce                      12
Beef turnover                       69, *69*
Beetroot and carrot salad           42, *42*
Bread, granary                      60, *61*

**C**
Carrot cake, spicy                  57, *57*
Carrot shapes                       28
Cauliflower, how to cook            44, *44*
Cauliflower salad                   44
Chicken with almonds                28, *29*
Chicken and bean salad              42, *42*
Chicken and pepper salad            68, *68*
Chicken with peppers                34, *35*
Chicken risotto, savoury            25, *25*
Chicken stock, basic                20
Chicken, breasts of                 64, *65*
Chicken with tarragon
  and strawberries                  66, *66*
Chilli con carne                    41, *41*
Chocolate mint mousse               16
Cornish fish pie                    31, *31*
Courgette and carrot
  quick-fry                         42, *42*
Cranberry jelly mould               46
Crunchy apple and
  cauliflower salad                 48, *48*
Cucumber chartreuse                 46
Cucumber and tomato
  salad                             42, *42*
Cucumber and yoghurt
  soup                              20, *21*

**D**
Dressings, mayonnaise               13
  orange                            13
  vinaigrette                       13, *13*
  yoghurt                           13, *13*

**F**
Fish, how to poach                  30, *30*
  in Tupperware                     32, *32*
Fish stock, basic                   20
Fruit Charlotte                     *52, 53*
Fruity cheese sticks                14, *15*

**G**
Garlic bread                        64, *65*
Granola                             62, *62*

Guacamole avocado dip               14, *15*

**H**
Honey and almond
  pudding                           36, *35*
Hot dill potato salad               49
Hummus                              15, *15*

**K**
Kedgeree                            62, *63*
Kiwi and prawn triangles            14, *15*

**L**
Leek, mushroom and
  Mozzarella plait                  *22, 23*
Lemon salmon in
  filo pastry                       16
Lollies, quick yoghurt              70, *70*
  Ribena and apple                  70

**M**
Marinated mushroom
  starter                           18, *18*
Mixed bean salad                    43, *43*
Mozarella and
  salami salad                      49
Muesli                              *62, 63*
Mushrooms in
  yoghurt dressing                  69, *69*

**O**
Onion and sour cream
  dip                               16
Oriental spare ribs                 28, *28*

**P**
Parma ham and fruit
  on sticks                         19, *19*
Pasta, how to cook                  40
Pasta and vegetable
  supper                            40
Pastry, wholemeal
  shortcrust                        22
  savoury plain                     22
  cheese                            22
  herb                              22
  horseradish                       22
Pâté and olive pastries             14, *15*
Pear and cinnamon
  crumble                           36, *37*
Piano pavlova                       55, *55*
Picnic ideas                        66, *66*
Pizza, bread base                   38
  pitta bread                       38
  pepperoni and chilli              38, *38*
  anchovy and vegetable             39, *39*
Potatoes, baked                     70, *70*
  cheesy tomato                     70, *70*
  cream cheese and bacon            70, *70*
Profiteroles                        51, *51*

**R**
Radish flowers                      28
Raspberry Swiss roll                58, *59*

Ribena and apple lollies            70, *70*
Rice, how to cook                   24, *24*
Rogan vegetable curry               45

**S**
Salads, apple cabbage               42, *42*
  beetroot and carrot               42, *42*
  cauliflower and fruit             44
  chicken and pepper                68, *68*
  French bean and
    chicken                         42, *42*
  mixed bean                        43, *43*
  Mozzarella and salami             49
  tomato and cucumber               42, *42*
Salmon, lemon, in filo
  pastry                            16
Salmon, how to poach                32, *32*
Sauces, easy white                  12, *13*
  béchamel                          12
  tomato                            13
  sweet and sour                    13, 27
Sausage and bread roll              68, *68*
Scones                              56, *56*
Seafood soup, special               20
Spare ribs, barbecue                65, *65*
  Oriental                          28, *28*
Spicy beef and kidney
  beans                             36
Spicy lamb with caraway
  dumplings                         34, *34*
Spinach and ricotta flan            22
Spring onion curls                  29
Strawberry gâteau                   54, *54*
Summer fruit cheesecake             16, *17*

**T**
Tandoori chicken kebabs             39, *38*
Taramasalata                        14, *15*
Tomato and cucumber
  salad                             42, *42*
Tomato roses                        28
Tomato sauce                        12, *13*
Trout, how to poach                 33
Tuna and basil salad                67, *67*
Tuna mousse                         18, *18*

**V**
Vegetable broth                     21, *21*
Vegetable fish terrine              46, *46*
Vegetable kebabs                    64, *64*
Vegetarian stir-fry                 43, *42*

**W**
Walnut torte                        50, *50*
White sauce, easy                   12, *13*
Wholemeal cookies                   *56, 57*
Winter spinach salad                49, *49*

**Y**
Yoghurt, home-made                  63, *63*
Yoghurt and mint dip                15